ABOUT THE AUTHORS

Eleanor Gaire is a graduate of the University of Limerick and The Marketing Institute of Ireland. Having worked in the corporate sector for 14 years, she now runs Storm Marketing and Design, a communications business. She has been involved with the Parents' Association and the Board of Management of her children's schools for the past eight years. She lives in Dublin with her husband and three children.

Oliver Mahon BL spent 20 years teaching in national schools, the last six as a school principal, before going into law. Given this background, he always had a strong interest in the law as it relates to education, and is the author of *Negligence and the Teacher* (1995); *The User's Guide to the Education Act* (2000); and *The Principal's Legal Handbook* (2002), as well as newspaper and magazine articles. He lectures widely to students and teachers on various aspects of education law as well as practicing as a barrister and has spoken on the topic on a number of radio programmes. At present he is simultaneously preparing the second edition of *Negligence and the Teacher* and writing the first supplement to *The Principal's Legal Handbook*. He lives in County Galway with his wife and two teenaged children.

PRIMARY OPTIONS

*How to Choose the Right School
for your Child . . . and Much More!*

Eleanor Gaire and Oliver Mahon

The Liffey Press

Published by
The Liffey Press
Ashbrook House
10 Main Street
Raheny, Dublin 5, Ireland
www.theliffeypress.com

A catalogue record of this book is
available from the British Library.

ISBN 1-904148-48-4

Printed in the Republic of Ireland by ColourBooks Ltd.

CONTENTS

ABOUT THE CONTRIBUTORS

Dr David J. Carey is the Coordinator of Special Education and Programme Development at the Froebel College of Education, Blackrock, Dublin. He lectures in special education and directs continuing education courses in special educational needs for pre-school, primary and secondary school teachers. Dr Carey directs a course for kindergarten teachers in Nairobi, Kenya, as part of the college's volunteer educational development work.

Dr Paul F. Conway is a graduate of St Patrick's College, Drum-condra, Dublin, and received his PhD in Educational Psychology from Michigan State University. Having taught primary school in Dublin for a number of years, he is currently a College Lecturer in the Education Department, University College Cork, as well as a Visiting Scholar at Michigan State University. He is co-editor of *Irish Educational Studies*, the journal of the Educational Studies Association of Ireland (www.esai.ie).

Dr Suzanne Guerin is a Lecturer with the Department of Psychology in University College Dublin. She has been involved in research with children for the past ten years and has explored issues such as bullying at school, understanding children's experiences, and special needs and disability. She has worked extensively with schools on the development of child-centred policies.

Dr Gemma Kiernan is a Lecturer with the School of Nursing in Dublin City University. She has previously worked both with the Centre for Early Childhood Development and Education located in St Patrick's College, Dublin, and with Barnardos. She has been involved in research on topics such as childhood illness, early childhood care and education and the impact of educational disadvantage.

Kim Pierce is Secretary of the Home Education Network, a voluntary group that supports home educators, raises awareness of home education and lobbies government on home education issues. Kim and her partner have three children aged 12, 10 and 5, all of whom have been home educated and have never been to school. She is a keen organic gardener and maintains a small orchard, the fruits of which her children enjoy!

ACKNOWLEDGEMENTS

The authors wish to acknowledge their gratitude to David Givens at The Liffey Press who responded immediately and enthusiastically when initially contacted about the idea for this book. We believe that his advice at the beginning to expand our scope has made it a far more useful book than had originally been planned.

We are grateful to the following people in their respective educational bodies for preparing and submitting overviews of their individual sectors: Fr Dan O'Connor (Catholic Primary Schools Management Association); Canon John McCullagh (Church of Ireland Board of Education); Colm Ó Dulacháin (Gaelscoileanna Teo); Deirdre Mangaoang (Educate Together); and Michael Troy (Association of Independent Junior Schools).

Having recognised that there was a need for expertise for a number of chapters, we were very fortunate to be able to secure support from the following: Dr Suzanne Guerin and Dr Gemma Kiernan who contributed the very insightful chapter on child development during the primary school years; Dr Paul Conway who wrote the chapter on the primary curriculum; and Dr David Carey for his complete up-to-date account of special needs education. All of these experts gave willing and freely of their time and professional experience, despite heavy work schedules and other commitments and for that we are extremely grateful. Many thanks also to Fionnuala Kilfeather of the National Parents Council Primary who contributed to the chapter on Parents' Organisations and to Kim Pierce who gave us an interesting and informative chapter on home education. Thanks also to Liz Gaire whose work in prompting justice and equality of access to education is an inspiration.

And finally to Brian Langan, our editor at The Liffey Press, whose skill in weaving sections together and making the whole book more cohesive and comprehensible is immeasurable. His patience towards the end was seriously tested but never doubted.

INTRODUCTION

Given that the great majority of readers will have passed through the Irish primary education system in the relatively recent past, and will have quite clear memories, whether good or bad, of the experience, what useful purpose can be served by reading a book such as this?

One of the major preoccupations of new parents (after sleep) is where to send their child to school. There was a time not so long ago when parents sent their children to the local primary school — possibly the same one they had attended — and there was very little choice.

There are several ways in which parents — even youthful ones whose own schooldays are not too far behind them — are likely to find that the system has changed. An obvious one is the growth in the options available to many more parents. As well as the regular national schools that have been providing the basic education to the children of the island since the early nineteenth century and which were, until fairly recently, the only option available for most families, there are now several other models available in many, although not all, parts of the state.

Parents may be considering sending their child or children to one of these "new" school types of which they may not have had personal experience; *Primary Options*, as its title suggests, attempts to survey the various models so as to give parents in this situation enough background information that they have some understanding of the type of school that they may be about to choose — even if it is only enough to enable them to ask useful questions before they finally make up their minds. In addition to comparing and contrasting these different models, the book examines many of the issues of concern to parents, issues that arise in all types of schools, including legislation, rights and responsibilities, admissions policies, curriculum, homework, child development, bullying, discipline, special educational needs, health and safety, parents' associations, home education and so on.

Parents have little comparable information and less time available to do the kind of in-depth research that they feel is necessary. At present there is no official source of information on the comparative performance of schools available to the public. There is no published research on the quality of teaching and standards achieved either in individual schools or in groups or types of schools. In the absence of solid up-to-date information, parents are left with the task of assessing what is on offer without the necessary criteria or tools. In an attempt to research different schools, parents are left to rely on the information volunteered by schools themselves along with the opinions of others. It must be said in defence of school boards and principals that it is not their role to "market" their school, as many factors which affect the standard of education rest with the Department of Education and Science.

One of the fundamental objectives of the Education Act 1998 is to promote the right of parents to send their children to a school of the parents' choice. It can be very frustrating for some parents, having done some research to be told that their first choice school is full and has a waiting list. The problem in some areas of the country where a range of options does exist is that there is great pressure on places and parents are having to consider their options not long after the baby is born. In these circumstances it is important to know your rights in relation to admission and what options you have.

Many parents of young children are living in new housing developments where the educational requirements for a growing population may not have been adequately planned. Many parts of our large cities and towns require new schools while in some rural areas populations are in decline and school enrolment is falling. Due to relocation and work commitments, many people have less contact with their immediate communities so that they have less local knowledge or neighbours with whom to consult. Often parents are working at some distance from their homes and their young children may be in care in crèches or pre-school outside their immediate communities.

Every year for a variety of reasons families move home, often requiring a move to a new school also. In 2000–01 approximately 20,000 children enrolled in ordinary classes in primary schools who had previously been enrolled in another national school within the state. This may seem like a very high proportion out of a total number of new enrolments in that year of approximately 80,000; however, the majority of those transferring would have been made up of boys or girls transferring from schools that have mixed classes from junior infants to first class and then are single sex up to sixth class.

Another way that the system has changed, and one that is more important although less obvious, is that in 1998 this state enacted the first general education statute since its foundation, and in so doing redesigned the landscape of education for everyone. The importance of the Education Act 1998 can hardly be overstated; in the opinion of the editors, it is the most important single development in Irish education in the twentieth century, and many would say since the establishment of the national schools in 1831. It is radical in the true meaning of that word, for its aim is nothing less than the creation of a new model for the delivery of education in Ireland at both primary and post-primary levels. In the course of doing this, it defines in statutory form for the first time the roles of the various parties involved in the delivery of education in recognised schools throughout the state. Formerly there was a degree of uncertainty and vagueness in the system as to what precisely was the responsibility of each, but now, as a result of the Act, all the parties — the Minister, school patrons, boards of management, principals and teachers and most significantly parents and students — now "know their place" in the system; in the case of parents they actually have a place, which was not the case before.

The Act conceives the delivery of education in recognised schools as being organised somewhat along the lines of a co-operative enterprise, with all parties working to a plan to enable the delivery of an appropriate education to every student in the system. This is quite a departure from the previous model, which was very much a directed one, with the directions being given at national level by the patrons and the Minister, and at local level by teachers and management, with little provision for consultation with those outside the system at any level. Perhaps the most telling feature of the reformative character of the 1998 Act is that, over six years after its passing, its effects are only beginning in many cases to be felt; at a guess, it will be several more years before the final results of its passing become apparent. Whether the new system, with all its carefully designed virtues, will work as well as or better than the old one with all its inherent faults is something that only time will tell, but for better or worse the world of Irish education was changed forever on the day before Christmas Eve 1998.

Important as it was, the 1998 Act was only the first of several recent legislative interventions by the Oireachtas in education. A new school attendance act had been promised for many years; it materialised in 2000 in the form of the Education (Welfare) Act, which aims to be much more than a mere attendance act and to address the problem not only of getting children into school but of enabling them to derive as much benefit as possible from being there. In the same year came the Equal Status Act 2000, which is not an education statute at all but nevertheless has enormously important implications for schools. Two more important enactments followed in 2001: the long-promised Teaching Council Act (which is at the time of writing in the course of being implemented), and the Vocational Education (Amendment) Act, a highly significant amendment to the corpus of legislation. The Ombudsman for Children Act followed in 2002, and an Amendment to the Data Protection Act in 2003 has the effect of bringing most schools within the ambit of this legislation for the first time. This is not all: the education of persons with special educational needs is now also to be regulated by statute; freedom of information legislation has now expanded to affect schools; and we are promised at some time in the future (this would be a most welcome development) an act to make specific provision for adult and second-chance education. In addition to these structural changes, what pupils learn and how they learn has also changed with the introduction of the new Primary School Curriculum in 1999, after a period of major review. All of this has taken place since the seminal act of 1998; no wonder that parents who have even recently left the education system are finding that they are behind the times.

WHAT THIS BOOK COVERS

This book is intended for Irish people who are approaching the primary school system for the first time as parents, and also for those who are considering a change of educational environment for their children. It will also be a good introduction for families who are moving to Ireland with children of school-going age. There are a growing number of children of non-nationals who have chosen to live in Ireland and who have no previous experience of our education system. This book will be useful in helping them understand the system and helping their children integrate successfully. While some of the book is specifically aimed at those new to the system, there is much of interest to *all* parents of primary school children.

Chapter 1 examines the Irish education system, and primary schools specifically, in terms of how they are organised, managed and funded. Much legislation has been introduced since most parents were last in school and the relevance and impact on the educational experience of this is covered. The rights and responsibilities of parents, children, schools and the state are outlined.

Chapter 2 looks at some of the important factors parents should consider when choosing a school for their child. The important issue of ethos is discussed in some detail, as for many parents it is the key issue in deciding on which school to choose.

Other important issues, such as proximity to home, facilities and extra-curricular activities are considered. The legal aspect of admission to schools is described in Chapter 2.

Some practical issues such as cost, length of school day, exemption from learning Irish, provision for non-English-speaking children and other useful topics are outlined in Chapter 3. This chapter also addresses in detail the question of safety in school.

At the start of the primary school cycle, parents start their precious four- and five-year-olds on the first steps of independence; eight years later, they are on the brink of adolescence. Children undergo enormous growth and development in the intervening years and in Chapter 4 Dr Suzanne Guerin and Dr Gemma Kiernan explore the changes parents can expect in their children during their primary years. Not all parents believe that their child is ready for school at four and Chapter 4 also sets out some guidelines as to how parents can judge their child's readiness for school. They also explore the factors parents should keep in mind when they begin to consider which type of school they might choose for their child.

Due to the way in which the education system has developed in Ireland, there are a number of different types of school. These are considerably different from each other in many ways, but in other respects they have a lot in common. In Chapter 5, the types of schools are explained and each governing body was invited to set out their ethos and what they represent to prospective parents.

After a long period of careful research and planning, the new Primary School Curriculum was launched in 1999 and has since then been gradually introduced into all schools. It is an extension of and different from the 1971 Curriculum both in content and emphasis. It also foresees a greater role for parents in contributing to their child's learning both at home and in school. In addition, the PSC encourages parents and the school to work together in supporting children's learning. In Chapter 6, Dr Paul Conway gives a detailed account of the various subject covered by the curriculum and the role of parents in supporting their children as learners. He also tackles the thorny issue of homework.

For some parents, the knowledge that their child will have special educational needs comes very quickly after birth while for others their children's needs only become apparent after they have started formal schooling. In either case, the priority for them is to locate the best possible services to maximise their child's potential. The provision of special education needs has received a great deal of attention lately in part due to some high profile cases which highlighted how much this issue has been neglected in the past. In a clear and helpful manner, Dr David Carey outlines the conditions that result in a child being defined as having a special education need and presents the significant factors affecting success in their schooling. This chapter is also recommended to parents whose children don't have a special need because it may give some insight into this area as more and more children with special needs are being catered for in mainstream classes.

For many, the idea of home schooling would be a daunting prospect and not likely to be undertaken lightly. There are in Ireland currently about 100 families where parents are providing for the education of their children at home. Despite the small numbers, it is a sector that is gaining ground, and in Chapter 8 Kim Pierce of the Home Education Network gives an interesting alternative perspective on the traditional approach. We also describe the legal requirements for those children under the Education (Welfare) Act 2000. Children being educated anywhere other than in a recognised school must be registered with the National Educational Welfare Board, who will carry out an assessment to ensure that a "certain minimum education is being provided".

How parents can and should get involved in their children's schools is covered in Chapter 9. The issue of communication between parents and school is crucial, and this chapter looks at parent–teacher meetings, and the importance of getting involved with the Parents' Association is also stressed. At a broader level, the National Parents Council is the representative body of parents and as such represents the views of parents on a variety of relevant boards such as the Educational Welfare Board and The National Council for Curriculum and Assessment.

Chapter 10 gathers together a number of issues that have become contentious in recent years. Bullying has always been an unwelcome part of school life, and the issue has now become a major problem in some schools. The related issue of discipline, and the complaints procedures in place should parents encounter a problem with the school, are also discussed here. Along with co-education, gender balance in teaching has become a hot topic, with just 17 per cent of teachers now being male. Finally, Ireland's increasingly multi-cultural nature is reflected in diversity in the classroom, and the chapter concludes with a look at what strategies schools have undertaken to accommodate and integrate those who are "different".

It should be noted that most of the text was written by ourselves, except where otherwise noted. Views expressed by contributors are personal opinions and may not necessarily reflect those of their respective organisations or those of the other authors. For convenience, the word "parent" is used throughout the book to refer to both parents and guardians.

In much of the research and literature on successful outcomes for pupils, a great deal of emphasis is placed on the involvement of parents in supporting their child in school. The climate for partnership between home and school continues to improve with both sides benefiting from greater openness, co-operation and involvement. With increasing pressures on home life and the complexity of rules and legislation affecting the school environment, it is hoped that this book will provide valuable information in helping parents to understand more about what goes on in school and how they can actively support their child's learning.

Eleanor Gaire
Oliver Mahon
February 2005

Chapter 1

STRUCTURE AND MANAGEMENT OF SCHOOLS

INTRODUCTION

How a school is structured and managed is of vital importance to how well it functions, which can have a huge bearing on the quality of education which your child receives. Yet many parents are unaware of exactly how their child's school is run; for them, the "public face" of the school is the physical buildings, the teachers and the principal. The ownership of the school, the structure of the board of management and the relationship between the school and the Department of Education and Science may not be high on parents' agendas, but all of these things can become important at various points in your child's education — especially if problems arise.

This chapter begins and ends with a look at parents' and children's rights — beginning with a look at what the Constitution has to say about schools and education, and finishing with an outline of some specific rights which parents have. In between are sections on school ownership (which is examined in more detail in Chapter 5 when discussing differences between school types); the functions of the school's patron and board of management; the responsibilities of the Department of Education and Science; and a brief look at the inspection system, and the concept of whole school evaluation, which is being phased in over the next few years.

THE RESPONSIBILITY OF THE STATE

The role and the responsibility of the state are clearly set out in relation to the provision of education in Ireland in Article 42 of *Bunreacht na hÉireann*, the Constitution of Ireland. Article 42 deals entirely with education, and it makes very clear that the primary responsibility for the provision of education lies with the family. The parents have both the right and the duty "to provide according to their means" for the education of their children. The article gives parents four options for arranging for the provision of this education: they may provide it in their own homes (what is often called "home education"), or in private schools, or in schools recognised by the state or established by the state. These rights are specifically acknowledged by the state, and the state is precluded from interfering to compel parents to send their children to any particular kind of school.

It follows from this that while education is compulsory in this country, school attendance is not. Parents may choose to discharge the duty to provide education themselves, in their own homes, and some parents do this (see Chapter 8); but for practical reasons the great majority opt for a school to provide this education for their children.

In order to enable the parents to do this, the state has a duty to provide for free primary education, which it does through an organised system of schools. The Department of Education and Science administers education nationally, funds schools, pays teachers and maintains inspectorial and administrative systems to enable education to take place locally. The investment by the state in education is in financial terms very great, and is growing all the time. As society becomes more developed and more complex, there is a greater demand and need for the provision of education, and so the education universe is, like the universe itself, constantly expanding.

The state also has a duty to guard what is called "the common good", and therefore Article 42 empowers the state to interfere in family arrangements to a strictly limited extent in relation to education. The state is specifically empowered to insist that children receive what is described in the Constitution as "a certain minimum education, moral, intellectual and social".

What precisely this means is not altogether easy to say. The Constitution was put in place in 1937, and Article 42 has never been amended since, and so will soon be 70 years old. The world of 1937 was a very different place from the world of 2007, and what would have been acceptable as "a certain minimum education" then would clearly not be adequate now. The phrase has never been precisely defined in law, which is in fact a good thing, as it is thus flexible enough to be expanded or adapted to take account of changes in society, technology and perceived educational need. Nobody in 1937 could, for instance, possibly have foreseen the emergence of information technology and its importance in everyday life, as evidenced by the presence of the computer as a ubiquitous tool in every workplace.

The second, and equally limited, way in which the Constitution empowers the state to interfere with the family's competence in the field of education is stated at the very end of Article 42. In situations where the parents have failed "for physical or moral reasons" to discharge their duty to provide for the education of their children, the state is enabled to step in and arrange the provision of education for the children. Again, this is done in its capacity "as guardian of the common good"; however, even in this extreme situation, the state's powers are restricted, as Article 42 closes by insisting that, in making up for the failure of the parents to make provision for the requisite education, the state must in all cases have regard for the rights of the child, who is after all at the receiving end of the education process.

It will be clear from the foregoing that the role of the state in the Irish education system is a strictly limited one. Parents are the primary educators with the right (and the duty, so it is not something that parents may opt out of) to provide for their children's education. The role and responsibility of the state is to provide the necessary support, such as functioning schools, to enable the parents to discharge their role. The state only becomes directly involved as an education provider in cases where the parents are either unable due to their circumstances to make the provision themselves, or utterly neglectful of their responsibilities.

The practical effect of this is that, in Ireland, unlike most other countries, most primary schools are owned by private bodies or organisations with an interest in the provision of education (see below). The various churches own and help to administer most of the country's primary schools, and other bodies and organisations, described more fully later in this book, own and administer most of the others. The Constitution is entirely happy with this, and indeed encourages it. Another part of Article 42 obliges the state not only to provide for free primary education, but also to try to aid "private and corporate educational initiative", so that the present position is in fact completely in harmony with the general constitutional scheme for the provision of primary education.

Elsewhere in the Constitution there is another important provision in relation to education of which parents should be aware. Article 44 deals with religion and the role of the state in relation to it, and as well as guaranteeing freedom to practise and profess religion, there is a further guarantee that is of significance, given the fact that most of our primary schools are owned and to an extent administered by the various churches. It is a provision to the effect that any child who attends any school that is in receipt of "public money" may do so without any compulsion to attend religious instruction at that school — an important guarantee for parents who, because of geographical factors may be compelled to cause their child to attend a school established by a denomination to whose tenets they do not subscribe. This issue is discussed in more detail in Chapter 5.

THE OWNERSHIP OF SCHOOLS

Schools in Ireland fall into two classes: recognised and unrecognised. *Recognised* means recognised by the Minister for Education and Science, and a school must fulfil certain conditions (set out in the Education Act 1998) before it can be recognised. (It is also possible for a recognised school to have its recognition withdrawn, but this would be a most unlikely eventuality; the consequences for such a school and its students and staff would be catastrophic.) The effect of recognition is that it brings a school within the operation of the various Acts relating to education and also enables its staff to be paid, and most of its costs to be met, by the state. *Unrecognised* schools are purely private and operate outside the remit of the Department of Education and Science completely.

To get a clear picture of the range of primary schools in Ireland, it is useful firstly to look at a few facts and figures. The present system consists of over 3,200 schools catering for over 440,000 children. There are over 22,000 teachers employed and the expenditure on education at primary level alone in 2002 was €1,853.1 million (see chart below).

Expenditure on Primary Education 2002 (Total €1,853.1)

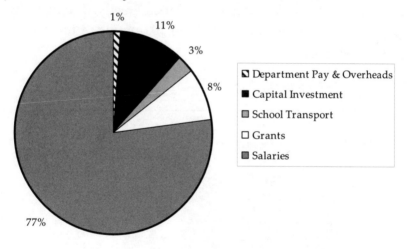

Source: Department of Education and Science Statistics.

As the chart below shows, of the total number of children the vast majority — over 424,000 — were pupils in ordinary classes with an additional 9,400 pupils with special needs accommodated in ordinary national schools. There were in addition nearly 7,000 pupils in special schools. Only 6,400 pupils attended private non-aided schools.

Number of Pupils per School Type (percentages)

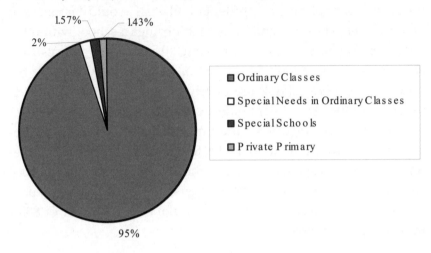

The size of schools, based on the number of enrolled pupils and the number of teachers employed, varies greatly. The majority of schools are small, having fewer than 100 pupils as the chart and table below show.

School Size by Number of Pupils

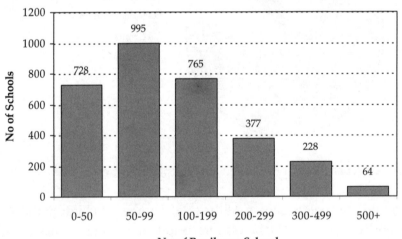

School Size

Pupil Size of School	0-50	50-99	100-199	200-299	300-499	500+	Total
No of Schools	728	995	765	377	228	64	3157
Total No of Teachers	1,554	3,843	5,510	4,748	4,137	1,681	21,470
Pupils	22,350	72,599	108,550	91,999	89,075	40,134	424,707
Average Pupil–Teacher Ratio	14.4	18.9	19.7	19.4	21.5	23.9	19.8
Average Class Size	15.3	21.5	24.6	25.3	26.9	29.4	24.2

The majority of schools in the Republic (3,104) are under the patronage of the Catholic bishops. There are about 200 schools under the patronage of the Protestant Churches, including 16 Presbyterian and one Methodist. The multi-denominational organisation Educate Together caters for over 5,000 children at 35 different schools (with a number of other schools proposed); and 47 gaelscoileanna are under the patronage of An Foras Pátrúnachta. (All gaelscoileanna in Gaeltacht areas, and the majority outside, are under the patronage of the local bishop.)

For local and historical reasons that, while no doubt important in their day, are largely forgotten now, a small number of schools were vested in departments of the state such as the OPW or the Department of Finance. In practical terms, this makes no difference to the way that they function.

There follows a brief account of the different kinds of primary schools in Ireland. These are looked at in more detail, under different headings, in Chapter 5.

Schools Owned by the Churches

Since Article 42 specifically enables "private and corporate" bodies to establish schools, and obliges the state to support this where it can, and since pursuant to Article 43 the ownership of private property is a constitutionally guaranteed right, it follows that, given the restricted role of the state in the education area, most primary schools are in private, not public ownership. This means that the plot of ground on which the school stands, and the school buildings themselves, are private property. (Many people have the mistaken impression that school buildings are somehow public places like, say, the public roads, and that anyone who feels like it has a right to enter them; this is not so.) As regards schools established by the various churches, these are almost invariably owned by the churches themselves, although the state pays the salaries of the teachers and also pays most of its running costs and upkeep through the system of grants, the amount of which vary with the size of the school.

Gaelscoileanna

There are actually two kinds of gaelscoil in existence, although from the point of view of the pupils who attend them and their parents there is no difference as regards education provided. One set consists of gaelscoileanna that are vested in the Minister of Education and Science and because of this are actually state schools. This set of schools has its own management authority, called An Foras Pátrúnachta na Scoileanna LánGhaeilge. The other set comprises gaelscoileanna, usually in Gaeltacht areas, that are vested in the local diocese, and so are not state schools, but are in fact identical to ordinary national schools and have the normal board of management appointed by the patron, except that of course they deliver an education through the medium of Irish. (The role of the school patron is dealt with more fully in the next section of this chapter.)

Model Schools

There are nine model schools still in existence. These, as the name implies, were originally established to be exemplars of best practice in pedagogy and administration, and were intended to have a role in introducing new teaching methods and enlightened management into the Irish education system generally (as well, of course, as teaching the pupils who attended them!). The intention was that the teachers in other schools would attend from time to time at these model establishments and, having observed the

latest teaching methods being demonstrated in the real-life setting, would carry back what they had learned and apply it in their
own schools, thus leading to a gradual spreading of expertise
throughout the system as a whole. For this reason, model schools
were to be strategically located around the country to ensure an
even distribution of these centres of excellence in instruction, with
each school acting as a catalyst of enlightenment and forward-
thinking in its own area. The in-service role of the model school
has long since been taken over by other forms of teacher training
and education, and it is not a disparagement to say that at this
stage the only way that these schools are "model" is in the name.
Because of their necessarily close ties to the Department of Education, these schools are state schools, having the Minister of Education as their patron, with an Inspector of the Department as the
chairperson of the board of management. From the point of view
of the pupils and their parents, there is no difference between attending a model school and any other kind of primary school.

Educate Together

Educate Together is the association of the patrons that adhere to the
Educate Together Charter. In this sector parents are the driving
force in the establishment of these schools and they have very significant participation in the patronage and management. The role
of the patron is occupied by a company, limited by guarantee,
whose members comprise the supporters of the school in the local
area. This membership generally consists of the parents, ex-parents
and prospective parents of children in the general community. This
company has charitable status and is governed by the Companies
Acts, which ensures that it is run in a fully accountable and democratic manner. In later years, once recognised, Educate Together
schools are owned by the Department of Education and Science.

Non-Aided Private Schools

Due to the fact that these schools are purely private enterprises
there is a wide variety of ownership structures. Some are owned

by religious orders, others by trustees and others by individuals or families.

Special Schools

Throughout the state there are some special schools, which as the name implies provide education for pupils with special needs. (Some pupils have educational needs, sometimes associated with a disability, that cannot be catered for in the regular primary school system.) These schools have a confusing variety of ownership; some are owned by Health Boards, some by the Department of Education, others by religious organisations or voluntary bodies set up to provide for a particular area of special need. See Chapter 7 for more on students with special education needs.

FUNCTIONS OF THE PATRON AND BOARD OF MANAGEMENT

The Patron

Every school is required by law to have a patron whose role and functions are stated in the Education Act 1998. It is probably unlikely that the patron will directly impact on the pupils or their parents, as the patron plays no part in the day-to-day running of the school. For the sake of completeness, here is a synopsis of the role and functions of the patron as set out in the Act.

Any person or group of persons may be the patron of the school. The Minister for Education and Science is required by law to keep a register of patrons of recognised schools, and the person or body whose name or names appear on this list is treated in law as the school patron and will be dealt with by the state as such. In order to effect a change of patron, it is necessary to apply to the Minister to make a change in the register.

In day-to-day terms, the most important function of the patron is to appoint the board of management of the school (see below). Each member of the board is appointed by the patron, and can if necessary be removed by the patron and replaced by another appointee. If necessary, the patron can dissolve the entire board. No one else — not even the Minister — can remove a board member or dissolve a board. The patron is required to formulate the *ethos* of the school; this word is not used anywhere in the 1998 Act, which uses the more cumbersome expression "characteristic spirit" instead, but the two expressions mean the same thing. (The ethos or characteristic spirit is very important in day-to-day terms and determines how the school and the teachers approach certain issues and will be dealt with more fully in Chapters 2 and 5.)

Apart from these two primary functions — appointing the board and determining the ethos — the patron largely plays a background role as regards the school, but the board of management is obliged to inform the patron of certain school activities.

Very frequently one person or body will be patron of several schools. Thus, for instance, the local Catholic bishop will normally be the patron of all Catholic schools in the diocese, and could not possibly be closely involved in all of them. The Minister for Education and Science is the patron of all the model schools. The parents are the patrons of Educate Together schools; while private schools might have an individual, family or trust as patron. At the post-primary level, the Vocational Education Committee is the patron of all the VEC-operated schools in that administrative area. Once a board of management has been appointed, the patron will not again be directly involved with the school during the lifetime of that board, except in exceptional circumstances.

The Board of Management

The board of management is far more likely than the patron to come into direct contact with pupils and their parents, and so is likely to be far more significant in day-to-day terms, and therefore the role and functions of boards of management will be considered here in greater detail.

Boards of management are a relatively recent phenomenon on the Irish primary school scene. When the system of national education was established early in the nineteenth century, it was done on the basis that each school would have an individual manager, living locally, who would ensure that the school operated in the way envisaged, would correspond with the central administrative authority (the Commissioners of National Education), receive and disburse grants and employ the teachers in the school who would be paid by the state. The system of the individual school manager, who performed the work voluntarily, survived until 1976, when the then Minister, Richard Burke TD, introduced the concept of the local board of management in place of the individual manager. This structure (a local board) has been modified slightly to make boards more representative, but is still in use.

The size of the board of management depends on the size of the school. For schools with a staff of more than one teacher, the board constitutes eight members, as follows:

1. Two direct nominees of the patron;

2. Two parents of children enrolled in the school (one mother and one father), elected by the general body of parents of children enrolled in the school;

3. The principal;

4. One other teacher on the staff of the school, elected by vote of the teaching staff;

5. Two extra members drawn from the wider community, proposed by the nominees listed at 1–4.

For one-teacher schools, the board constitutes the following:

1. One direct nominee of the patron;

2. The principal;

3. One parent, elected from and by parents of pupils enrolled in the school;

4. One extra member drawn from the wider community, proposed by the nominees listed at 1–3.

There are strict procedures in place for the election of the parents' representatives and at least ten days' notice must be give of a meeting to hold an election. Any parent with a child enrolled in the school can go forward for election. The current boards were appointed in November 2004 and will run for four years.

The board of management has numerous functions in relation to its school. Its members act without payment (or even expenses) and perform a vital administrative function on behalf of the state, the local community and the school patron. Each member is appointed for a four-year term by the school's patron. Once validly constituted, the board becomes a legal "person", and may perform all the legal functions of a person, such as entering into contracts in respect of the school (such as building contracts or contracts the purchase of land), can sue (and be sued) in its own name, and employs teachers and other members of the school staff. (It is the board of management, not the Department of Education and Science, that is the employer of the teachers, although, somewhat confusingly, they are paid by the state, not the board.) The members of the board have a statutory immunity from being sued in respect of their work on the board done in good faith in pursuance of the Act, and so it is the board itself, and not the individuals who are members of the board, which would be named as the defendant in any legal action against the school.

The primary duty of the board, clearly stated in the 1998 Act, is "to manage the school on behalf of the patron and for the benefit of the students and their parents" and "to provide or cause to be provided an appropriate education for each student at the school". In discharging these duties the board is required to act at all times in accordance with the policies determined by the Minister. The board therefore owes duties in three directions at the same time: to the school patron, to the students and their parents and to the Minister.

As regards the patron, the principal duty of the board is to uphold the ethos or characteristic spirit of the school. In addition, there are duties to consult with and keep the patron informed of certain aspects of the operation of the school. By and large, the board will not have frequent dealings with the patron in normal circumstances.

As regards the students and their parents, the principal duty is to provide an appropriate education for each student at the school. This education should be appropriate to the abilities and needs of the students, and this in some cases gives rise to problems. The 1998 Act requires schools to use their "available resources" to first identify and then provide for "the educational needs of all students". The problem is that the resources available can and do vary greatly from school to school, and teachers will be the first to point this out. Generally, although this is not invariably the case, the bigger the school the greater the amount of funding available, and therefore more resources can be marshalled to meet the needs of the students. Schools in large urban areas generally find it easier to gain access to support systems than those in remote rural areas. This can be particularly evident when it comes to recruiting staff to work in small schools.

Boards that are not discharging their functions properly can be dissolved. Only the patron who appointed the board can dissolve it. Thus a board that failed to perform its statutory duty to uphold the ethos of the school can be dissolved by the patron; there is a formal process of notification and warning to enable the board to "mend its ways" before this can be done. An individual board member can be removed by the patron following a similar process.

As part of its obligation to manage the school "for the benefit of the students and their parents", the board is required to perform certain subsidiary functions. One of these is the keeping of proper financial accounts showing income and expenditure, which have to be audited yearly. Schools can acquire funds from a variety of sources: grants from the state, funds raised by parents' associations, rental income from school facilities and occasionally donations and gifts. All these funds must be accounted for as income. Parents have a limited right to inspect school accounts: limited, that is, to monies provided to the school from public funds.

Another of the board's subsidiary functions is the preparation and publication to students and their parents of a variety of school policies. The list of these policies is being added to all the time, but at present the most significant, from a parent's point of view, are the code of behaviour, the anti-bullying code, the admission statement and the school plan. (Another important policy document is the school's safety statement, which is a requirement not of education legislation but of legislation relating to safety in the workplace.) Some of these will be dealt with elsewhere in this book — the admissions policy in Chapter 2; the safety statement in Chapter 3, and the code of behaviour and anti-bullying policy in Chapter 10 — but the preparation and circulation of the school plan is a significant function of the board that relates directly to parents and students, and is worth considering briefly here.

The 1998 Education Act obliges a board to prepare, and circulate to the patron, parents and staff, a school plan which must state the objectives of the school "relating to equality of access to and participation in the school", and how the school proposes to achieve these objectives. Specifically, the means of access and participation of those with special needs have to be set out, and the plan must follow guidelines given by the Minister for the preparation of such plans, and it must be "regularly reviewed and updated". In addition to this, there is a duty on a board to establish procedures for informing parents of "matters relating to the operation and performance of the school". A board may do this by whatever means it chooses, but there is a specific option given to a board of producing a report "on the operation and performance of the school". If a report is produced, it must be circulated to parents and teachers and other staff (and to a student council in the case of second-level schools). The objectives of the school are to be set by the principal, under the directions of the board and in consultation with the teachers, parents and the students where appropriate, and the principal is required to monitor the achievement of those objectives.

As regards the Minister, the board is obliged to do its business in accordance with state policy as determined by the Minister "from time to time". It is required to act at all times in accordance with all Acts and instruments of the national parliament and comply with directions of the Minister. It must also use grants and other resources efficiently while having regard to "the principles and requirements of a democratic society" and it is obliged to promote respect for social, linguistic and religious diversity, while making "reasonable provision" for pupils with special needs or who have a disability. (There is a carefully worded definition of "disability" in the 1998 Act.) The board would not (except in certain very limited circumstances as stated in the Act) have an input into the curriculum of the school, which is prescribed by the Minister, and the Minister also may make regulations governing many aspects of school life such as the admission of students, the qualifications of teachers, the length of the school year, week or day and the maintenance and equipment of schools; therefore the board's authority and responsibility are by no means unlimited.

In addition, boards have many functions under the various Acts in relation to schools that are too numerous to set out here, although some of them will be referred to elsewhere in this book. Members of boards are offered a certain amount of training, which is normally organised by the patron of the school, but in view of the fact that the role of boards is constantly being enlarged, more training is needed. Remarkably, the funding for this training was withdrawn by the last Minister and has not yet (at the time of writing) been reinstated.

The Principal

The role and functions of the principal of the modern school is far-ranging, extensive and varied. Apart from the leadership role in guiding the staff and implementing rules and policies, the principal has overall responsibility for the day-to-day activities of the school. In addition the principal has a role in ensuring the quality of teaching, planning work on the basis of the integrated curriculum, arranging for regular assessment of the pupils and ensuring good communication between ordinary class teachers and learning support teachers. The principal's role in relation to parents is in creating a climate of openness whereby parents not only feel welcome to discuss the progress of their child but also that they may through their association collaborate on the development of relevant school policies. As in any organisation, the leadership role the principal plays cannot be underestimated. An effective leader should be able to articulate a clear vision of what the school stands for.

RESPONSIBILITIES OF THE DEPARTMENT OF EDUCATION

Although, as we have seen, most Irish primary schools are in private ownership, the Department of Education exercises an enormous amount of authority over the education system generally, which has been significantly enlarged by recent legislation. It is specifically the responsibility of the Minister to ensure that there is available to every person in the state a "level and quality of education" appropriate to that person's abilities and needs. The Minister determines education policy and plans education provision. To enable education to be delivered through schools, the Minister provides essential funding for schools (including the payment of staff) and monitors, through the Inspectorate of the DES, the quality of the education delivered. It is the duty of the state to vindicate the constitutional rights of the citizen, and one of these is the right to education. A famous decision of the Supreme Court in the case of *Crowley v Ireland* stressed the significance of the preposition "for" in the clause "the state shall provide for free primary education" in Article 42, and held that by putting in place the administrative systems to deliver education through schools, the state had done what the Constitution requires of it. The 1998 Act obliges the Minister to provide, as well as the necessary funding, appropriate support services for schools, parents and students (including students who have special needs), to lease land (or buildings) to persons or groups for the establishment of schools, and to provide support services through Irish to schools where these are requested. (In doing these things, the Minister must at all times give effect to the constitutional rights of children, including those children who have special needs.) Furthermore, the Minister is obliged to set up a planning and advisory body to facilitate teaching through Irish, and a committee to advise on policies and strategies to address the issue of educational disadvantage.

The Minister also has muscle in relation to the delivery of education that can be exercised in instances where the Minister is unhappy that the schools are operating in the way that is envisaged by the DES. Boards of management, as we have seen, are obliged to act in accordance with ministerial policy; what happens where a board fails or refuses to do so? We have already seen that only the patron may remove a board member or dissolve a board. However, the 1998 Act empowers the Minister to require the patron to dissolve a board for stated reasons, and the patron must comply with this request. However the exercise by the Minister of this power is restricted to situations where the board's functions are not being effectively discharged, where a board "wilfully" fails to comply with any order, direction or regulation of the Minister, or where a board fails to comply with a court order.

Clearly, therefore, the Minister does not lack the means to ensure that the system is run in the way that the state desires.

THE INSPECTORATE AND WHOLE SCHOOL EVALUATION[1]

The role and functions of the Inspectorate are covered by Part III Section 13 of the Education Act 1998. The Inspectorate's role can be broadly divided into two main areas: the evaluation of the educational system; and the provision of advice to the educational system and policy makers. Some of the main functions of the Inspectorate, as they relate to pupils, parents and the effectiveness of schools, are as follows:

- To support and advise recognised schools, centres of education and teachers on matters relating to the provision of education;

- To evaluate the organisation and operation of schools and the quality and effectiveness of the education provided in those schools, including the quality of teaching and effectiveness of individual teachers;

- To conduct assessments of the educational needs of students in recognised schools and advise students, their parents and the school in relation to the educational developments of those students;

---

[1] Some material in this section is taken from the Department of Education and Science; the Education Act 1998; and the CPSMA Board Members Handbook 2004.

- To evaluate the quality and effectiveness of the provision of education in the state, including comparison with international practice and standards;

- In consultation with parents to assess the psychological needs of students in recognised schools and to advise those students, their parents and the schools in relation to the educational and psychological development of such students;

- To advise recognised schools on policies and strategies for the education of children with special educational needs.

In its role in the evaluation of quality and effectiveness in the primary school sector, the Inspectorate uses a number of different approaches:

- School self-evaluation;

- Extensive support for school development planning;

- Teacher in-career development and dedicated support services in the context of ongoing curricular change and development;

- School-designed or teacher-designed assessment and reporting to parents;

- Use of standardised assessment instruments;

- External evaluation of schools by the Inspectorate;

- Programme evaluations by the Inspectorate focusing on aspects of curriculum provision.

The Inspectorate contributes to quality assurance at primary level by inspecting schools, inspecting the work of individual teachers and by carrying out inspections of different aspects of the system. Schools are inspected approximately every six or seven years and includes an evaluation of all aspects of teaching, learning and assessment, school planning, the work of the school board of management, as well as the school's accommodation and resources.

At present, the evaluation report is discussed in draft format with the principal, teaching staff and the chairperson of the board of management before it is forwarded to the Department. There is no provision for this report to be made available to present or prospective parents (except the two parents' representatives on the board of management). An application to have these school evaluation reports made more widely available under the Freedom of Information Act succeeded in the High Court.

Whole School Evaluation

Following discussion with the education partners, including teachers' organisations, parents' groups and school management authorities, and following an initial pilot project, *whole school evaluation* was introduced on a phased basis in the school year 2003/4. The difference in WSE is that it will give a high degree of priority to the quality of teaching and learning, of school management and school planning and the inspections will be carried out with two inspectors working together. WSE will cover all aspects of the curriculum and will focus on the school as a whole.

The evaluations under WSE will include:

- Pre-evaluation meetings between the inspectors and the principal, teachers and members of the school's board of management;

- A meeting between inspectors and the officers of the parents' association;

- School and classroom visits, during which inspectors visit and observe in classrooms, interact with students, interact with teachers, and examine school planning documentation and teachers' written preparation;

- Preparation of a draft report by the inspection team;

- Post-inspection meetings with the principal, school staff and the representatives of the board of management.

It is intended that the final WSE reports will be important documents in the context of school development planning. In addition they will contribute to broader system development by providing information which can inform the discussion and modification of education policy. In accordance with Section 53(a) of the Education Act 1998 they will not contain "any information which would enable the compilation of information (that is not otherwise available to the general public) in relation to the comparative performance of schools in respect of the academic achievement of students enrolled therein".

The National Parents Council (Primary) has called for the inclusion of the evaluation of individual teachers in the inspection and in the final reports and that the information should be made available to parents and prospective parents. That notwithstanding, the WSE report should contain valuable information of interest to all the school partners.

If whole school evaluation reports were available to prospective parents, they would form a valuable but not entire basis for evaluating school choice. At the very least, they would provide solid information based on professional inspections across a range of criteria. However, it is probable that if the Department was to be compelled to publish results of individual reports, it would also change the way reporting is done. This issue is likely to be a source of much more debate before it is finalised.

LEGAL RIGHTS OF PARENTS AND CHILDREN

We have already seen that parents have constitutional rights in relation to education, such as the right to choose how to provide education for their children, and that children also have constitutional rights in this area. In addition, both parents and children have legal rights conferred on them by various statutes. The problem is that these rights are scattered throughout the various Acts rather than being tidily gathered together in one place, and so it is not easy to discover exactly what they are. Even if you take the trouble to read the Acts, it is still not easy to identify all of your rights. Some are clearly stated, such as the right of parents to send their child to the school of the parents' choice; others are not stated and have to be deduced from other provisions. For instance, a duty on a board of management to circulate copies of the school plan to parents confers a corresponding right on those parents to receive it.

In addition to the rights of individual parents, an association of parents also has rights. Parents' associations are specifically provided in the 1998 Act with certain entitlements; these rights are rights of the association and should not be confused with the rights that all parents have as individuals. The role and rights of the parents' association and those of the National Parents Council will be dealt with in Chapter 9.

A selection of the most important rights of parents and children drawn from various Acts is set out below for reference. Unfortunately, there can be no guarantee that these lists of rights are as comprehensive as one would like. One reason for this is that the High Court can, when a case related to the school system comes before it, identify and declare rights that up to that point had never been stated before, or can clarify rights of which we know. A good example of this process can be seen in the case, already referred to, of *Crowley v. Ireland*, where the judge who heard the case in the High Court, Mr Justice McMahon, stated that the duty of the state in Article 42 to provide for free primary education conferred a corresponding right on children to receive it. This judgment established that there is a constitutional right to education, as the Constitution itself does not actually state this right. Another reason why the list may be incomplete is that it is not always clear from the wording of an Act that a right exists, and it often needs a judgment of the High Court to clarify matters.

There is yet another reason why this list should be treated with care. Others besides parents and children also have rights and these too have to be given due respect. For instance, the patron has the right to determine the ethos of the school, and this is not something that any other party — parents, teachers, the board of management, even the Minister — can interfere with. The right of a parent to send a child to the school of the parent's choice has to be balanced against the right of the patron to maintain the ethos of the school and the right of the Minister to see that resources are used efficiently and effectively.

The list below also does not include rights relating to such areas as discipline, complaints, religious education, special needs, etc., all of which are dealt with in greater detail elsewhere in the book.

For all these reasons, the list of rights of parents and children has to be treated judiciously. Very few, if any, rights are absolute, no matter whose rights they are. The following list of rights is intended for the guidance of parents to help them manage their children's education, rather than as a weapon to be brandished at the first hint of a disagreement. Finally, for ease of reference and general intelligibility, the rights have been classified under headings which try to identify areas of general concern to parents and their children.

Parental Options for Education

As we saw above, Article 42 of the Constitution gives parents four options in discharging their duty to provide for their children's education. The law on school attendance, which is now contained in the Education (Welfare) Act 2000, has to follow this constitutional principle and so parents have the right to choose whether to opt for education at home, in a private school, in a school recognised by the state or a school established by the state. To ensure that the right of the child to receive education is protected, the Act has a mechanism to allow the Minister to send inspectors to check on the quality of education provided for the child in the home (see Chapter 8). In recognised schools, the quality is monitored by the school inspectorial system in the usual way. In private schools, the quality of the school itself can be monitored by the DES inspectorate, and there are elaborate mechanisms to address the situation where the education provided is found to be unsatisfactory. Parents who opt out of the recognised school system are required to register their children with the DES. The details of this registration system are described briefly in Chapter 8; parents who are contemplating either the home school or private (i.e.

unrecognised) school option would be well advised to contact the DES for information before committing themselves, as well as studying sections 14 to 16 of the Welfare Act.

Admission to Schools

Admission to recognised schools, which in the past was quite an informal process (parents simply brought their children to the school and signed them in), has now been greatly formalised as a result of recent legislation, and the whole area is now quite complex. Every recognised school is now required to have a formal admissions policy, which has to be published by the board of management. The content of these policies is considered in more detail in Chapter 2, as they are quite elaborate and contain more than a bare statement on admissions. As regards rights of parents, boards of management and persons concerned in implementing the 1998 Act (e.g. teachers) are required to promote the rights of the parents to send their children to the school of their choice, but they must also have regard to the rights of the patron and the state in regard to using resources efficiently. The board is required to maintain an admission policy that makes the school as accessible to students as possible and that respects the right of parents to have their children attend the school of their parents' choice.

Rights Relating to Recognition Issues

It is possible for a recognised school to have its recognition withdrawn by the Minister, just as it is possible for the Minister to confer recognition as a school on an existing or proposed "educational establishment", to borrow an expression from the Equal Status Act 2000. Just as the conferring of recognition brings a school within the aegis of the DES, the withdrawal of recognition would be a catastrophic event for most schools. The most immediate effect would be a total cessation of all state funding, as only recognised schools may receive public money. Very few schools could survive such an event and parents have a right to advanced notice where the Minister is of the opinion that recognition should be withdrawn. They then (along with the patron and the teachers) have three months to make representations to the Minister before recognition can be withdrawn. If this does happen then the students have a right to have alternative and appropriate facilities for their education put in place by the Minister. In practice, this is only ever likely to happen in situations where a declining population reduces pupil numbers below the level of viability of the school, and there are established procedures in place to manage these situations when they occur, so it is not usually an area of great concern for parents, although the sight of abandoned school buildings throughout the countryside testifies to the fact that populations do shrink and schools do go out of existence.

NEW SCHOOLS: ESTABLISHMENT AND RECOGNITION

Under Section 10 of the Education Act 1998, the Minister may from time to time designate a school or a proposed school as a recognised school. The criteria for recognition include:

- Evidence that the proposed school meets a need that cannot reasonably be met within the existing provision.

- The local community must be consulted in advance.

- The patron has been registered as such by the Minister for Education and Science.

- A board of management will be appointed in accordance with the requirements of the DES.

- The *Rules for National Schools* will be complied with.

- The proposed school has a minimum initial enrolment of 17 junior infants and a minimum projected of 51 pupils for the third year of operation.

- All pre-enrolled pupils are at least four years of age on 30 September of the year in which the school is due to commence operation.

- The school will comply with all relevant legislation in relation to buildings and health and safety.

- The school will follow the Primary School Curriculum of the DES.

- The school will employ recognised primary school teachers.

New primary school applications are assessed by the New Schools Advisory Committee (NSAC) which is an independent advisory group made up of a range of interested parties including representatives from the National Parents Council, Educate Together, Gaelscoileanna and the DES. The NSAC consults with interested parties and advises the Minister. Schools that have their applications rejected can appeal to an independent appeals committee.

In the past, the patrons of denominational, multi-denominational and special schools supplied and continued to own the site on which schools were established. Following changes in funding arrangements the state will supply and own the sites for new schools subject to the competing needs of other primary schools.

In the initial stages, the patron of the proposed school is responsible for securing suitable accommodation. Only when the new school demonstrates viability and secures permanent recognition does the school become eligible for capital funding.

Schools that have to rent accommodation and are granted permanent recognition are paid grant-aid of 95 per cent of any reasonable rent. Schools that have temporary recognition get 75 per cent rent subsidy. In the case of new building for recognised schools, there is now a ceiling of €63,487 which the patron has to provide towards the cost.

For further information, contact the School Planning Section, Planning and Building Unit, DES, Portlaoise Rd., Tullamore, County Offaly. For more on how to establish a gaelscoil, visit the website www.gaelscoileanna.ie. On how to organise a Start-Up Group, see www.educatetogether.ie.

Chapter 2

WHAT TO LOOK FOR IN A SCHOOL

PARENTS' PRIORITIES FOR THEIR CHILDREN

Each parent's search for a good school will probably be influenced by their own experience of school either negatively or positively and one should keep in mind how valid or not these predispositions are in the current task.

The Marino Institute of Education carried out a survey in 1997 to gain an understanding of how pupils, parents and teachers viewed school values.[1] Parents were asked to rank ten items according to the most important outcome they wanted for their child. The results were interesting:

1. Being a well-rounded person

2. Having respect for other people

3. Getting a good job

4. Being well-disciplined

5. Having Christian values

6. Having an ethic of hard work

7. Going to university

8. Having a concern for social justice

9. Being good at music/the arts

10. Being good at sports.

---

[1] Catherine Furlong and Luke Monahan (2000), *School Culture and Ethos*, Marino Institute of Education.

The results showed that by far the most important item that parents want for their children was being a well-rounded person, followed by having respect for other people. It is clear from this that parents in general take a broad view of the role of school life in the development of their child's full potential. Where they may have some difficulty is in assessing and predicting what impact different types of school will have on that outcome.

One of the difficulties for parents, apart from the lack of comparable information, is being able to define exactly what it is they are looking for. Parents very often start with the idea of a "good" school but find it difficult to articulate the criteria they will use in their assessment and what weighting they will give different aspects of what they perceive to be on offer. It is important to have some yardstick against which you might compare different schools and to avoid superficial judgements. In its booklet *Developing a School Plan: Guidelines for Primary Schools* the DES list the following attributes as important features of effective schools:

- Purposeful leadership by the principal

- Curriculum planning and development

- Appropriate communication structures

- Teacher/classroom preparation

- Intellectually challenging teaching

- An environment in the classroom that is conducive to learning

- A positive climate

- Parental involvement

- Assessment and record keeping

- Consistency in the implementation of agreed policies.

These are not tangible attributes that can easily be assessed in a quick visit to a school but they do give some insight into what in the long term defines a "good school". This, along with an evaluation of your priorities in terms of ethos, facilities and resources will help in making your assessment.

ETHOS

Individual schools or types of schools very often define themselves by their ethos or characteristic spirit. In the Education Act 1998, the characteristic spirit of a particular school is determined by the "cultural, educational, moral, religious, social, linguistic, and spiritual values and traditions which inform and are characteristic of the objectives and conduct of the school". It appears that in the education statutes the use of "ethos" was carefully avoided, perhaps because in the minds of many people the word has strong religious connotations, whereas the phrase "characteristic spirit" is more neutral without denominational overtones. Indeed the Act goes to some lengths to assert that the ethos of the school need not be denominational, and that schools that are avowedly secular can also have a valid ethos. Apart from the obvious definitions of religious denomination, co-ed or single sex, rural or urban, large or small, old or newly established, there exists a set of values and practices which permeate all aspects of the school and its relationships within its community.

It is very easy for a school board to publish a worthy mission statement that espouses inclusiveness, equality, progressiveness, a holistic approach to the development of each child as an individual and an openness in its management of its relationships with its stakeholders. It is much more difficult to endeavour to implement these ideals in the daily interactions between teachers, pupils, parents and management. The task for parents is to decide whether or not to accept the written statement of the ethos or aims of the school and then find out how faithfully the aspirations are carried through the policies, priorities and procedures of the management and the attitudes of the staff in embodying those principles.

Ethos is a complex, ever-evolving concept that transmits values and informs aims and objectives. In an educational setting it should inform the school's philosophy and underpin a set of guiding values and culture that give unity and cohesiveness to a school community.

This is why it is necessary to look beyond the narrow definitions of school types. Not all Catholic schools are the same, in the same way that not all Protestant schools or Gaelscoileanna are the same. While two schools with a shared religious philosophy may be similar, they will differ in other ways due to the fact that ethos is dynamic and evolves, and the extent of adherence to the original founding principle will naturally depend on how well successive school communities propagate and communicate those shared values. At Educate Together schools and Gaelscoileanna, there are founding ethical and educational principles that translate into policies which guide the day-to-day running of their schools. School types, and the ethos generally associated with each type, are discussed in greater detail in Chapter 5.

The culture in each school will be different because the people are different and the rules, traditions, environment, past experiences and problems faced all have a bearing on how the members of the school community see themselves and how they believe others see them. The challenge for parents is to match their child with a school where they can share the same beliefs and aspirations for the future.

Legal Aspects of Ethos

The patron of the school determines the ethos of that school, as discussed in Chapter 1. The board of management is legally obliged to uphold that ethos, and is accountable to the patron for this. As a necessary consequence of this provision, the patron can remove a board member or dissolve the entire board if the school's ethos is not being properly upheld.

The practical effect of this for parents and children is that no one other than the patron can form or vary the ethos of the school, and so when parents choose to enrol their children in a school, they must take the ethos of the school as they find it. Occasionally, parents find that they are unhappy with the ethos of the school in which they have placed their children, and seek to vary it. Unless the patron is agreeable, this is not possible; not even the Minister has any role in varying the ethos of a school. There is a presumption in law of long standing that when parents choose to enrol their children in a particular school they are accepting the characteristics of that school; if they find them unpalatable, they should then opt for a different school or a different way of providing education for their children.

This does not mean, however, that parents have no rights at all in this area. As we have already seen, there is a constitutional right for any child not to have religious instruction in any school that is in receipt of state funds. This would of course also extend to religious practices, and so, for example, a child of one faith, or indeed no faith, who is attending a denominational school of another faith, cannot be compelled to attend either the religious instruction, or take part in the religious practice, of that faith. In addition to this constitutional right, there is also the legal right, already referred to, that allows a parent to withdraw a child from instruction in any subject which is contrary to the conscience of the parent. It is important to note that this right is not confined to religious instruction, but extends to all subjects. This matter is dealt with more comprehensively in Chapter 8, in the context of home education.

Parents should also be aware that, although they may not share in the ethos of the school, they still have a legal right to have their children attend that school, and indeed it is quiet common, for educational or other reasons, for parents to cause their children to attend a school in whose ethos neither the parents nor children share. This issue is dealt with in section 7 of the Equal Status Act 2000, where it is clearly stated that the ethos of the school cannot be used as a pretext for a point-blank refusal to admit a student who does not subscribe to that ethos. However where the purpose of the school is to promote religious values, a school is allowed to admit pupils of its own denominations ahead of those not of that denomination; see "Admission to Schools" later in this chapter.

LOOKING LOCALLY FIRST

While the issue of ethos is an important one for many parents, it is not the only criterion in choosing a school. There are very compelling reasons to start your search with the school that is closest to your home. Firstly, when children start primary school they can find the day quite long and tiring, even if they have previously been in a pre-school or crèche. Very often they are in a class with a lot more pupils than they have been used to and the demands on their concentration is much greater. Therefore any increase in their journey to and from school should be avoided.

Your nearest school is most likely to be your parish/community school and there is a greater opportunity for being involved with those around you when your child goes to the local school. The chances are that school-going children in your neighbourhood are also attending the local school and this gives both you and your child an opportunity to make friends in the community. Your child will have playmates close to home and they will have a greater sense of security and of connectedness to the world around them.

On a very practical level, it also gives parents, guardians or minders a greater opportunity to share trips to and from school and you will have more support around when the inevitable delays and hold-ups happen.

Attending a school close to home will also give children the possibility of taking part in after-school activities which may not always start directly after formal classes finish. A short trip back to school to take part in a sport or music class may not seem like much in the beginning but, if down the line you have more than one child in the school finishing at different times, you may find that your time from 1.30 pm onwards is a constant round of dropping off, waiting and collecting. If you get involved with your school's Parents' Association, meetings are often held in the evenings and this could involve more trips.

As your child gets older there may be an opportunity to walk or cycle safely to school, giving them a sense of independence and some exercise. For parents working outside the home there is the additional consideration of after-school care. The options are a school with integrated after-school care (mostly provided at a few private schools); or an arrangement whereby an after-school facility collects your child from school and minds him/her until you arrive home; or an arrangement with a minder to care for your child in their home or yours after school. Whichever arrangement you opt for, it must also cover holiday time, occasional days off, in-service days for teachers (usually about six per year), days when your child might be sick and unable to go to school and the very odd emergency when a school may have to close early (e.g. failure of the heating system or very bad weather).

Contact your local school and ask what the enrolment policy is. Policies may vary from school to school. Find out if there are generally a lot more applicants than places available and if you safely meet the entry requirements. Ask what the procedures for applying are and when you should apply. Some schools will only accept applicants in the year previous to the year in which the child is expected to start others may be oversubscribed and in those cases it is important to have applied as early as possible. There is an extended explanation on the legal aspects of admission to schools later in this chapter.

You may have a preference for either mixed (coeducational) schooling or single-sex schooling, which may or may not be influenced by your own experience in school. Unless you live in a large urban area, it is unlikely that you will have a choice, given that fewer than ten per cent of primary schools are now single-sex schools. There are some schools that are mixed up to first class and then are single sex from there to sixth class. The dilemma in such schools is to judge the relative benefits of having some time in a mixed environment over the disruption of moving to a different school in second class. This question is also dealt with in Chapter 4.

VISITING SCHOOLS

For all schools, local or otherwise, ask if it is possible to visit the school on an open day or during the evening. It also may be possible to visit during the school day, which gives a better "flavour" of what the school is like. However, you will obviously be restricted from visiting classrooms, for instance, during the working day. Also, the role of principal is a very demanding job nowadays, so it is courteous to ask for an appointment to meet with him or her.

You will get some clues as to how a school is run by its appearance — not so much in the state of the building, because lack of investment has meant that some school buildings may be in an appalling physical state, but in terms of how well a school is maintained. Does the place look clean and bright or is it litter-strewn with little evidence of pride of place? There is enormous variety in the quality of school buildings ranging from sub-standard to new architect-designed accommodation. Some boards of management and principals struggle with prefab buildings long past their normal life while they await approval for replace-ment buildings. However, new buildings and shiny equipment are no guarantee of a good teaching environment.

When you get to the school you can judge how the pupils be-have. Does the place seem orderly? This creates an environment conducive to learning. In the absence of hard facts, people are al-ways on the lookout for clues as to how their child might fit in. Find out how big the junior infants class(es) will be. That alone is only somewhat relevant. A competent teacher will cope fine with a class of even 30 co-operative five-year-olds. However, if disci-pline is a problem and the teacher is not in control, even a class with a lot fewer pupils will struggle.

Ask if all of the teachers are fully qualified. In recent years, due to shortages some schools were left in the position of employ-ing people who were not qualified. Even if you have no suspi-cions about your child's ability, it is always worth finding out about availability of resource teaching for pupils who may have difficulties with Maths or English.

If your child is interested in sport, find out what activities are included in the PE curriculum and what other sports are offered as optional after-school activities. At what age do they start? Is the emphasis on competitive sports or is there a fair attempt to en-courage participation, regardless of competence?

If your child has a special talent or need does the school have a strength in that area? What opportunities does the school provide for allowing the children to be creative? How are music and drama catered for? Do the children participate in school plays or concerts? Is there evidence of children's creative work nicely dis-played or are walls kept exclusively for academic work?

What are the rules on uniform, discipline and homework? The school should have written policies to cover these. Most schools would not give homework until senior infants or first class. Chapter 6 not only covers what your child will be learning in school, but also how you can support him/her with homework.

Find out how active the Parents' Association is. Well-run schools actively encourage the positive involvement of parents and this is a sign that there is an open and co-operative atmosphere.

Ask parents with children already attending the school about their experiences of the school; also ask how their children are getting on and, if there are problems, ask sensitively why this is so. Don't always be put off by negative comments because some people's expectations may be unrealistic or they may have particular problems with a child which has created a bias against the school's point of view. However, a pattern of non-committal or negative responses should be a cause for concern.

Finally, a note of caution; it is a disturbing development in recent years that the demand for places in certain secondary schools is such that parents are not only placing their children's names on a list for primary school but they are also reserving places in secondary school. Some primary schools are attached to secondary ones and in most cases children in the primary section would have an automatic right to a place in the senior school. Other secondary schools that do not have a primary section may have a feeder arrangement with a primary school in an area and this is important to know if you are fixed on a particular secondary school.

FACILITIES

This is probably one of the areas where there is greatest disparity between schools right across the country. The conditions in substandard schools can include some or all of the following: cramped conditions in classrooms, leaking roofs, inadequate toilet facilities for pupils and staff, no separate accommodation for principal or secretary, no library facilities, little or no playing areas, little or no equipment for PE, art, science or music or schools that are dispersed amongst a number of buildings. At the other end of the scale, there are purpose-built schools which have been well-designed with toilets attached to each classroom, bright PE halls, on-campus playing pitches, separate and well-stocked libraries and up-to-date computer facilities. Most schools in the country fall somewhere along the scale of inadequate to satisfactory facilities. It is more of a problem in some of the start-up schools and older schools needing refurbishment or replacement. Some newer schools are housed in makeshift or adapted buildings while they await department funding for purpose-built accommodation. When community groups come together to start a new school there is a long and difficult task of fund-raising and lobbying in order to get up and running. Some people feel that they are willing to make this commitment in order to provide the type of school for their own children and others that would otherwise not be available. On the other hand, others feel that it is an unfair burden on their children and themselves to provide a service that is supposed to be enshrined in the Constitution and provided by the state.

Some of the independent schools can offer such facilities as extended schools days, hot lunches or the option of inclusive after-school care. This may be very attractive to families who need full time childcare and it avoids them having to arrange separate care after school. Where the school takes care of extra-curricular sports, music and drama there is less work for parents to ferry children from school to these activities.

ADMISSION TO SCHOOLS

In the past the admission of a child to a school was a simple and straightforward matter. Once the child reached the legally permitted age of attendance (which is currently four), he or she was entitled to enrol in a national school. Enrolment itself was uncomplicated also: the parent simple marched the child to the school and handed him or her in; the teacher noted a few details, and the child was thereupon a member of the school community, once his or her name was entered in the school's register. Since classes were so much larger in the past, there was rarely a question of a school being unable to admit a child.

All this has greatly changed in recent years, and the whole business of having a child admitted to a school has been greatly formalised by legislation. The general principle is that a parent is entitled to have their child enrolled in the school of the parent's choice. This, however, is not an absolute right; it has to be balanced against the right of the patron (discussed in Chapter 1) to maintain the ethos of the school, as well the efficient use of resources. Boards of management are obliged to put in place and maintain an admissions policy that allows for maximum accessibility for pupils to schools, and they are also required to draw up a formal policy document relating to the admission and participation by pupils in the school. This document must be published, and it is required to respect the right of parents to send their children to the school of the parents' choice as well as "the principles and requirements of a democratic society" and to respect social diversity while at the same time having "regard to the efficient use of resources" but at the same time to use those resources "to make reasonable provision and accommodation" for those with special needs. Clearly any document that can accomplish all that will be a complex one. Having said this, it should be noticed that this is not the same as saying that a child will necessarily be admitted to the school, as there may well be perfectly valid reasons why the school is unable to accept all the children who apply.

The actual decision to admit or not is one for the board of management, although in normal circumstances the board leaves the actually handling of the details of admission to the principal. The parent is obliged to provide the board with whatever information may be prescribed by the Minister, and then the board is obliged to make a decision either to admit or refuse to admit the child, and convey this decision to the parent in writing, within 21 days. A school may only refuse to admit a child in accordance with the provisions of its own admissions policy, referred to above. For this reason, most schools set out in the admissions policy the grounds on which they may have to decline to admit a child who applies.

For most primary schools throughout the state, the admission of a child into any class is a routine procedure with the minimum of formality. The reason for this is that most schools are not under pressure of space, and indeed in many cases the reverse is the case. For some schools, however, space is at a premium; this usually happens in the vicinity of expanding towns or suburbs, where the population has grown but the number of schools has stayed the same. In the absence of new schools coming on-stream, the existing schools cope as best they can by adding extensions or installing "temporary" structures (which often end up having a working life far in excess of what was ever intended), but eventually the space runs out, and then a school is forced to be selective as regards entry. This is the point where the trouble begins.

Lack of space is a perfectly valid reason for a school to decline to admit a child. Clearly there is a point at which overcrowding becomes an issue, on health and safety grounds as well as on educational ones. In these circumstances schools are often forced to define their catchment areas in order to identify those children whose applications will be prioritised. Schools have to do this in a way that is fair, consistent and transparent, and schools usually set out a descending order of priorities. Most of these lists start by giving priority to a child who already has a sibling in the school; this is done out of consideration for the constitutionally protected family unit. The children of staff members are often placed next, for the same reasons. Proximity to the school is usually next; sometimes, this is defined as residence within a parish or parishes, and sometimes in terms of a straight line on a map. Finally, any remaining places are usually allocated on a first-come-first-served basis. Other factors may also come into play, such as religion (in a denominational school) or the age of the child (with five- or six-year-olds being given preference over four-year-olds).

All of these are straightforward and generally cause little difficulty. However, there are some other situations where a board may decline to accept an application, which may bring it into dispute with a parent. One of these relates to the school's code of behaviour, the contents of which are discussed in more detail in Chapter 10. The relevant section of the Education (Welfare) Act 2000 provides that the principal may require, as a condition of registering a child in the school, that the parents declare in writing that they accept the code of behaviour and that they will make "all reasonable efforts" to ensure that their child complies with it. It would then be open to the board to decline to admit the child of parents who refused to sign this declaration to the school, provided that this had been provided for in the school's admission policy. (This is a somewhat theoretical issue, as parents do not in fact refuse to sign these declarations.)

Admission of Pupils with Special Needs

A much more live issue for schools is where children are presented for enrolment who have such special needs that the school cannot meet them out of its own resources. The issue of special needs is dealt with from an educational perspective in Chapter 7. Here, we will outline the options for parents where such difficulties arise.

How should a school deal with an application from parents of a child who has a disability? Clearly an assessment of the needs of the child is essential, together with an assessment of the resources that the school can deploy to meet them. Given that the school has a duty to provide an appropriate education to every pupil in the school, and this includes students with special needs, boards of managements and teachers sometimes feel that if a pupil is admitted whose needs are so special that the school cannot provide for them, the school will be in breach of its statutory duty. This seldom happens, and most pupils' special needs can be catered for reasonably successfully, but occasionally a prospective pupil is presented whose needs are so unusual that the school cannot provide the appropriate education that the 1998 Act demands. In these circumstances, many schools will accept the application of the pupil but will seek to defer the actual attendance while the requisite supports are put in place. In some cases, alterations to the buildings may be required, such as installing ramps instead of steps or lavatory and washing facilities for pupils with physical disabilities; in other cases, since disability takes many forms, specialist staff may have to be recruited, or teaching hours made available in the form of one-to-one tuition. These arrangements take time and usually cost money, which has to be provided by the Department of Education and Science, as schools themselves do not usually have discretionary funds available to meet situations such as these. In the meantime, the child may be left in a sort of limbo, which is most unsatisfactory for the parents, the child and the school alike.

The newly established National Council for Special Education (NCSE) will act as a central organising agency for the resourcing of special educational needs, acting at a local level through Special Educational Needs Organisers (SENOs). It is hoped that, in time, these new structures will streamline the process of assessing and approving resources for special educational needs. The roles of the NCSE and the SENOs are outlined in Chapter 7.

However, when there is a serious and insurmountable mismatch between the available resources and the needs, the school is in a difficult situation. Does the board admit the child, knowing that it will be in breach of its statutory obligation to provide education appropriate to the needs and abilities of the pupil, and that such a failure may leave it liable to a variety of consequences, none of them pleasant? Or does it decline to admit the child, thus causing inconvenience to the family and perhaps hardship to the child who may be compelled to travel a long distance to a school where his or her needs can be met, and possibly leading to an appeal (discussed below) under section 29 of the 1998 Act? In this situation there are no winners, no matter which decision is taken.

What can a parent do in either of these situations? There may be a number of options open to both parents and school, involving negotiation, mediation, etc. However, these are not provided for under the legislation, and generally operate at a local level. Should such options fail, and should the parents still feel determined to pursue the matter, as a last resort there is a legal route available to them.

In a situation where a school has admitted a child but has failed, or is unable, to provide an appropriate education to him or her, a parent may complain to the Children's Ombudsman pursuant to the Ombudsman for Children Act 2002. This Act contains a mechanism whereby a parent can complain to the Ombudsman for Children (not to be confused with the "ordinary" Ombudsman, who has been in place since 1980) in a situation where a school has taken an administrative decision that is not in the best interests of, or may have been damaging to, a child. The Ombudsman may investigate the decision and the reasons for taking it, and publish a report on the situation, which will go to, among others, the Houses of the Oireachtas and the DES. No school will wish to be named and criticised in such a report. This might arise in a situation where a child had a need for, say, five hours of resource teaching each week but the school, due to a lack of resources, was only in a position to provide, say, two hours, given that resource teachers usually have to provide services to several pupils during the week, and the demand usually seems to outstrip the supply. While it is probably unlikely that a complaint to the Ombudsman would succeed in the circumstances, and would not benefit the relationship between home and school, it is an option that a frustrated parent may feel driven to explore.

In the event of a board of management declining to admit a child to a school, the procedure is more straightforward. Section 29 of the 1998 Act gives the parents of a child a right of appeal in such circumstances to the Secretary General of the DES. A section 29 appeal does not involve courts or lawyers. Appeals are heard in private and so, unlike court hearings, the details will not appear in the newspapers, and there is no charge to parents for the appeal. (However, should the parents choose to employ a lawyer there is no mechanism for the awarding of costs if the appeal is successful, so the parents must pay their own costs.) The rule is that the board must give its decision in writing to the parent within 21 days of the application, and then the parent has 42 days to lodge an appeal against this decision with the Secretary General. The procedure to be followed can be summarised as follows: the parties are first urged to resolve the issues by negotiation among themselves; if this fails, a facilitator/mediator is appointed who tries to guide them to a solution, and if this also fails, a for-

mal hearing before an Appeals Committee appointed by the Secretary General takes place. The decision of such a committee is
final and binding on the parties.

One final issue relating to the legalities in this area relates to
the duty of a school to identify the educational needs of students.
In some cases, where the special educational need may be psychological, this will require testing by an educational psychologist, a
service which is now usually provided by NEPS — The National
Educational Psychological Service. Because of the constitutional
protection of the family unit in this country, any examination of a
child — medical, dental or psychological — has always needed the
written consent of a parent or guardian before it can take place,
and very occasionally parents have refused to sign the consent
form. This of course puts a school in a difficulty, as the examination cannot take place without it, and the school is then prevented
from identifying the needs of the student as it is legally obliged to
do. Happily, the Education for Persons with Special Educational
Needs Act 2004 addresses this problem, by providing a mechanism by which an application to the Circuit Court may be made to
set aside the refusal of the parent to sign the consent and in these
circumstances the Court may make whatever order is considered
to be in the best interests of the child. The most likely order would
of course be that the child should be assessed.

IN CONCLUSION

In the final analysis your choice of school for your child may be
the result of a reasonable assessment of all of the factors and a
judgement of where your child will be happy and a trust in your
own knowledge of your child and your concern for their future.

Finally, when you have chosen the school and secured a place
for your child, respect the different choices of others. It is not a
competition and most responsible parents will have made their
own choice for the best reasons for their child, as you did for yours.

Chapter 3

PRACTICAL ISSUES

SAFETY AND SECURITY IN SCHOOLS

This is a very big topic, and space in this book does not allow for it to be dealt with in any great detail, and so what follows is a general overview of the area. Each school is required to develop its own safety policy, suited to its own circumstances and needs.

The board of management is responsible for the overall management of the school, and school safety and security are part of this general responsibility. The various education acts do not deal with this area of school life except as regards school discipline, and then only to a limited extent. Instead the area is covered by the general law of safety in the workplace. The rules of school safety law come principally from two sources: statute law (i.e. laws made by the Oireachtas); and also from the decisions given by judges hearing individual cases in the Superior Courts (i.e. the High Court and the Supreme Court) which are usually referred to as "judge-made law". I will deal briefly with each of these sources.

School Safety and Security under Statute Law

The principal statute in regard to schools is the Safety Health and Welfare at Work Act 1989. The 1989 Act is a general workplace safety act, designed to apply to every sort of workplace, and does not mention schools, students or teachers at all. However, schools, although not specifically mentioned, are included by virtue of the fact that "place of work" is defined as any place where work is carried on, and specifically includes a premises. The Act sets out

the duties and responsibilities of employers towards their employees in relation principally to their safety in and about the
workplace. Schools are somewhat unusual workplaces in that, although they are certainly places of work, most of those present
during the working day are children, who of course are not employees, and so while the provisions of the Act do apply directly
to the staff, who are employees of the board of management, they
only apply indirectly to the students.

Only some sections of the Act are of particular significance for
parents. Section 7 obliges every employer to manage his business
so as to ensure that persons present on the premises who are not
employees (e.g. children in a school) are not put at risk as regards
their safety or health. Safe entry and exit are also the responsibility of the employer, i.e. the board of management.

An important section from the point of view of parents and
students is section 9, which places certain duties in relation to
safety, health and welfare on the shoulders of the employees,
which of course in the case of schools means principally the
teachers, although other school staff such as caretakers would also
be included. Employees are obliged to take reasonable care, not
only of their own safety, health and welfare, but also that of other
people (which in a school would mean mainly the pupils) who
may be affected by their acts or omissions in the course of their
work. (As this duty ties in with the duties under judge-made law,
it will be dealt with in that section below.) There is also in this section a duty on employees to report to the school authorities any
defect in the premises, the school equipment or the management
and organisation of the workplace that might cause a danger to
safety, health or welfare, once they become aware of it, and the
board have a duty to rectify the situation. Between them, these
two sections (7 and 9) go a long way towards providing for the
safety of the children while at school.

Another significant provision of the 1989 Act which will be of
interest to parents is the requirement that every place of work
must have a written safety statement, which has to set out how
the safety, health and welfare of employees is to be secured. The

safety statement is required to identify any hazards in the work-place, then assess the risks arising from these hazards, and finally to put in place arrangements to protect the safety of those employed there. (In a school, a simple example of a hazard would be the main fuse board, which creates a risk of electrocution. The way of guarding against the risks would be by making it inaccessible, for example by placing it in a locked cabinet.) All the hazards have to be identified, assessed and either eliminated, which is the ideal, or minimised, where elimination is impossible. Once the safety statement is drawn up, it becomes the duty of the board to bring it to the attention of the employees and to any other persons (which in the case of a school would obviously include pupils and parents) who may be affected by it. Schools normally do this by making a copy available for inspection, on request; some schools make extracts of the most important parts and present them in the form of a poster on notice boards. Parents should note that they are only entitled to inspect the safety statement; they are not entitled to be given a copy to keep.

There is no provision in the Act in relation to school security; again this is the responsibility of the board of management. Irish schools have traditionally been easily accessed, and until relatively recently the funds did not run to the employment of secretaries or receptionists. (Many small rural primary schools still do not have a secretary/receptionist, or may only have one on a part-time basis.) In practice, matters of day-to-day security fall on the shoulders of the principal, assisted by the teachers and the caretaker if the school is lucky enough to have one. Happily, security during the school day has not been a pressing issue for Irish primary schools. The main problems tend to arise at weekends, when the kinds of equipment found in modern schools (CD players, computers, musical instruments, TVs, videos and the like) make schools targets for petty criminals. For some schools there is an ongoing problem with vandalism. These matters do not usually have much direct impact on parents and pupils, unless such serious damage is done that the working of the school is disrupted as a result. The problems are usually addressed through surveillance and alarm systems in larger schools, and lock-and-key remedies in smaller ones.

School Safety under Judge-made Law

Most of the legal rules relating to the safety of children in school or on school activities are to be found, not in the various education acts or the safety acts, but in the decisions given by judges in cases where pupils have sued schools or teachers on foot of injuries sustained in the classroom, the school yard, the school building or on activities organised or supervised by the school staff. These rules are not easily accessed even by lawyers, as they are scattered through many decisions given by different judges at different times. In addition, it is not always easy to discern a hard-and-fast-rule that is of general application, as each decision only relates to the particular case in which it is given. However, there have been enough lawsuits against schools in relation to injuries sustained by pupils, that it is possible to make certain broad statements of fact in relation to the area. Again, this aspect of the safety issue is far too large to be addressed in anything remotely like its entirety here, and so the following is a synopsis that we hope is enough to sketch out the general picture.

When a parent hands over a child to a school to be educated, the school also assumes a responsibility to take reasonable care of that child for the period that the child is in its care. In legal terms, the parent, who owes the child a "duty of care" — a duty to take care of him or her — in effect passes this duty on temporarily to the teachers who take the child into their charge. Parents owe their child a duty of care because they are his or her parents; the teachers owe the child a duty of care because it is passed over to them along with the child. Teachers have no choice but to accept this duty, and it is not something that they can choose to have or not; the duty is a legal duty, imposed by law. (This is not a situation that only applies to teachers; we all have duties of care at different times, and no more than the teacher with the child, we have to accept them. Thus when we get behind the wheel of a car, we have a motorist's duty of care towards every other road-user; a doctor has a duty of care towards the patients; a solicitor owes a duty of care to the clients.) The teacher's duty is normally formed when the care of the child passes from the parent to the school, and normally ends when the parent reclaims the child from the school. During the period that the child is in the care of the school, the teacher is in effect a substitute for the parent, and this fact has become so well accepted in law that it has been elevated to the status of a legal doctrine, known as the doctrine of *in loco parentis*, which translates literally as "in the place of the parent". Of course, the teacher does not truly become *in loco parentis* in every respect; these are some duties of the natural parent that do not (except perhaps in the most exceptional circumstances) ever pass to the teacher. For instance, parents have a legal duty to feed, clothe and provide for their children; teachers merely have the duty to protect them from harm and guard them against foreseeable risks and, of course, to provide for their education.

The duty of care varies with the age of the child, the general rule being the younger the child, the higher the duty. (This is true for both parents and teachers.) In terms of the primary school, it means that teachers need to be most careful of junior infants, and as the children progress through the school, the duty of care gradually diminishes as they get older. (For anyone who has ever worked, either as a parent or as a teacher, with small children, this is only a matter of common sense.) However, as long as there is a pupil–teacher relationship, there is always some duty of care, no matter what the age of the child.

The general rule that the extent of the duty of care diminishes as the ages of the children increase is not, however, true in every case; some children need a degree of care in excess of what would be appropriate to others of the same age. Anything that makes a child more than usually vulnerable increases the duty of care for both parent and teacher, and a child with a disability is generally owed a higher-than-usual duty of care, which varies with the nature and degree of severity of the disability in question.

Saying that teachers owe a duty of care similar to that of a parent raises the question: which sort of parent? Parents vary just like everyone else, and some are more protective, more prudent and more watchful than others. The law has taken the very sensible view that the duty of care owed is equivalent to that of a reasonably prudent parent, and so an obsessive level of care is not required, nor indeed would it be approved by the courts. In a number of cases, judges have tried to balance the necessity of providing adequate care with the undesirable practice of stultifying children by over-protectiveness. This is particularly relevant in relation to school playgrounds, which have always been seen by judges as places where children can learn lessons about themselves and each other that are just as valuable — perhaps even more valuable — than what they learn at their desks. Courts have traditionally frowned upon attempts by adults to make school playgrounds so safe, by restricting pupil's freedom to run and play, that no accidents can ever occur. It is inevitable that there will be collisions, bumps and injuries (most of which are happily very minor) in any school playground where a large number of school children are busily at play, particularly when play for small children almost invariably involves running about. The exercise of the teacher's duty of care in these circumstances means ensuring that unsuitable, dangerous or inappropriate games are not played, or that appropriate games are not played in an inappropriate way, or that play does not extend to inherently dangerous activities such as climbing on walls and roofs, or that unsuitable and inappropriate objects are not brought into the yard by children who cannot, because of their immaturity, be expected to understand the consequences that may follow. In such circumstances teachers have both the right and the duty to stop the play, to confiscate a potentially dangerous object or to do anything else that is necessary to make the situation safe.

Another important factor to be considered when trying to compare the teacher's duty of care to that of a parent is that the teacher must discharge that duty in relation to far more children (classrooms of 30 children and more, schoolyards of far more than this) than any parent is ever called upon to deal with in a family setting, and so judges have also stressed that the teacher's quasi-parental duty of care has to be considered in the context of a school.

Many injuries sustained by pupils in school are occasioned in one way or another by fellow pupils. Some, but certainly not all, of these can be prevented by schools putting in place a regime that treats safety as a priority, and so teachers, as part of their general duty of care, are under a duty to put in place a system of adequate school discipline, as a means of guarding against foreseeable risks. The school disciplinary system is usually reduced to the form of clearly stated school rules which are then given to children and parents in writing. Rules on their own are of no use unless enforced, and so a duty of enforcement of school rules is a part of a teacher's general duty of care. When rules are broken there has to be some form of effective sanction for the breach, as otherwise the children, who are too young to understand that the rules are there for their benefit, would not obey them.

Parents can greatly assist schools by reading the rules with their children, and explaining the thinking behind each rule, as these matters, while obvious to an adult, will not be apparent to a child. For instance, a strict rule saying that pupils must not cycle in the school yard might at first sight appear merely arbitrary or officious, until it is explained that it is designed to prevent injuries, both to the cyclists and to those on foot with whom they may collide. There are many other ways in which an effective regime of school discipline is a part of the general duty of care, both inside and outside school buildings and on school outings. It is particularly important in dealing with bullying and related matters.

As both bullying and school discipline have both become of late particularly live issues, they are dealt with as separate topics in Chapter 10, but it would be misleading not to point out here that school safety and school discipline are not two separate and unrelated topics as they might easily appear, and that teachers are legally obliged to have a disciplinary system in place and enforce it for the good of the pupils. The details of this will be set out more fully in Chapter 10.

Even in the most careful and well-conducted schools, pupils will inevitably have accidents. In primary schools statistics show that most of these occur in the school playground, during one of the breaks between classes. (Most schools take two breaks during the day, although a small number take three. As each of these breaks is timetabled and allowed for, the actual teaching time is the same for all pupils, irrespective of the number of breaks.) One of these breaks will normally be the lunch break, and will be considerably longer then what is called "short break". Curiously enough, such statistics as are to hand indicate that more accidents occur during the shorter break; perhaps pupils play more vigorously at this time. The most common kinds of injuries in primary schools are grazes and cuts, followed by bruises, nosebleeds and sprains — almost all minor, and few needing the attention of a doctor or nurse. The most common causes of injury have been found to be slips, falls and collisions in the great majority of cases, followed by sport-related injuries.[1]

A very small number of injuries will be serious enough to cause the parents of a child to consider suing for compensation, and recognised schools are legally obliged to have a policy of insurance in place to deal with these instances, which happily are few. In these cases it is the board of management of the school that is normally the defendant, since the board has overall responsibility for what goes on in school. However, a word of caution is appropriate here. There is no compensation to be got from a court for what might be called a "pure" accident. Unless it can be shown by evidence that the injury was somehow caused by the action or inaction of a teacher or other staff member, a court cannot award compensation. Some children sustain injuries, even serious injuries — and this happens at home as well as at school — which are not anyone's fault, and our system of law only allows compensation to be awarded by a court in cases where fault is established. The result of this is that some children who have

---

[1] These statements are based on the findings of a survey on school injuries conducted some years ago by the Church and General Insurance Company, which insures most primary schools throughout the state.

genuine injuries can get nothing by way of compensation, since they cannot satisfy the court that the injury was in some way the result of the negligence of an employee of the board of management. In order to fill this gap, and ensure that there is at least a modest sum available in respect of routine injuries, there is a variety of low-cost insurance schemes on offer to parents and most schools facilitate parents by making these available through the school. By buying cover under one of these schemes parents can ensure that there is some compensation available in respect of injuries sustained both at home and in school. Queries on the details and costs of these, and other matters related to safety at school, should be addressed to the school.

LENGTH OF DAY AND SCHOOL YEAR

School must start no later than 9.30am and formal instruction must begin no later than 9.50am.There should be four hours and ten minutes secular instruction during the day, which can be reduced by one hour for infant classes. In the *Rules for National Schools* there is provision for 20 minutes for assembly (roll-call, etc.) and 30 minutes religious instruction each day. A lunch-break of 30 minutes must be included along with another ten-minute break or two five-minute breaks. In total the amount of time in school is five hours and 40 minutes (usually from first class upwards).

The social partnership agreement 2003–2005 *Sustaining Progress* included a clause for the first time on the standardisation of the school year. The holiday periods up to 2007–2008 have been agreed and published.

Parents are strongly discouraged from taking their children out of school for holidays outside the agreed official holiday periods. Under the Education (Welfare) Act 2000, schools are obliged to notify the National Educational Welfare Board if a child is absent from school for 20 days or more. Tempting and understandable as it is to avail of cheaper off-peak holidays or to accommodate other circumstances in the family, it is disruptive to the work of the class and the teacher to have pupils coming and going at different times.

Children do miss out on schoolwork and the school is not obliged to make up for lost time.

Every school must be in operation for a minimum of 183 days unless in very exceptional circumstances (e.g. failure of the heating system). Any decision to close a school for whatever reason must be taken by the board of management.

SCHOOL TRANSPORT

Pupils attending their nearest appropriate national school who have to travel more than two miles from home will qualify for free transport on a scheduled bus service or school bus if either is available. In some cases particularly in rural areas there will be insufficient pupils to justify provision of a school bus. Where this arises parents will receive a grant to assist with the cost of transporting the child. This Scheme D grant, funded by the Department of Education and Science, is paid retrospectively each year based on vouched attendance figures. If you are considering sending your child to a particular school and transport is a problem, check whether the school's bus service covers the area where you live (or want to live).

EXEMPTION FROM LEARNING IRISH

There are circumstances under which pupils may be exempt from learning Irish as part of the curriculum. They are as follows (these conditions are slightly abbreviated and the full text may be found in the *Rules for National Schools* or may be requested from a principal):

a) Pupils whose primary education up to 11 was received in Northern Ireland or outside Ireland.

b) Pupils who were previously enrolled as recognised pupils in national schools who are being re-enrolled after a period spent abroad, provided that at least three years have elapsed since the previous enrolment in the state and the pupil is at least 11 years of age on re-enrolment.

c) Pupils with a specific learning disability.

d) Pupils with a general learning disability due to serious intellectual impairment.

e) Pupils with a general learning disability due to serious sensory impairment.

f) Pupils from abroad who have no understanding of English when enrolled, who would be required to study one language only, Irish or English (see below).

g) Children of foreigners who are diplomatic or consular representatives in Ireland.

h) Children from other countries in whose case the Minister is satisfied that they are resident in this country as political refugees.

NON-ENGLISH SPEAKING PUPILS IN PRIMARY SCHOOLS

Primary schools that have more than 15 non-national pupils are entitled to an additional temporary teacher for a period of two years specifically to develop those pupils' English capability. A grant is given in the instance of schools in which between four and 14 non-English speaking pupils are enrolled. Where there are three or fewer such pupils, no additional resources are allocated and schools are expected to provide for those pupils from within their existing resources. (See also the section on diversity in Chapter 10.)

HEALTH SERVICES THROUGH SCHOOL

Health Boards provide children attending recognised (not including independent) schools health examinations and screenings for certain conditions, free of charge. Dental, optical and aural treatment and appliances for defects noticed at the school examinations. In addition vaccinations and immunisations are organised through school. The Health Board, through the school, must obtain permission from parents to treat or vaccinate their children.

Administration of Medicines

A child who is obviously sick should not be sent to school. It is not only unfair to the sick child but also to the other children in the school and to the staff. Parents should be particularly vigilant with regard to contagious diseases and should inform the school if your child has been diagnosed with anything that might be of concern to other children and staff. It is inevitable that young children will pick up sicknesses from each other and this is a fact of life for which you must be prepared.

There are, however, circumstances whereby a child has recovered sufficiently from an illness to return to school even though they may still be undergoing a course of medication. There are also children who live with conditions which do not prevent them from attending school and who are on long-term medication (e.g. diabetics or asthmatics). No teacher can be required to administer medicines or drugs to a pupil. If, at the request of a parent, a teacher is willing to administer medicine, they are required to seek authorisation from the board of management. The INTO and the CPSMA have agreed and published a set of guidelines that should be followed in the circumstances and the parent will be requested to sign an indemnity agreement to cover the teacher, principal and school arising from any claims arising from the administration of or failure to administer the medicine.

In emergencies, teachers should do no more than is necessary and appropriate to relieve extreme distress or prevent further and otherwise irreparable harm. If any of the staff are trained in First Aid, they should be consulted, but qualified medical treatment should be secured at the earliest opportunity.

RETENTION OF PUPILS IN SAME GRADE

The Department's policy in relation to a pupil repeating a year is that it should only be allowed for educational purposes and only in exceptional circumstances. In such circumstances, a consultation should take place between the principal, class teacher, resource teacher and the parents and if it is deemed that a pupil would benefit from repeating a grade a decision in that regard can be taken. A record of the decision must be recorded and a plan drawn up as to what new approach to the child's education will be used and what its expected benefits will be.

This regulation has implications for parents who may be in doubt as to the possibility of repeating a year if their child started in school at the younger end of the four to six age scale. At present, the minimum legal age is four years, which is very low by European standards, where the norm is six or thereabouts. The reason for this is the lack of a system of pre-schools in this country, and so children are allowed to start "real" school earlier, to compensate. Remarkably, at one time the legal starting age was three years. In the past it was felt that if a child had started too young and was not settling in or making satisfactory progress, they could easily repeat a year without too much fuss. This suggests that parents who have a doubt about their child's readiness for starting school before they are five should wait for the following year.

In the words of one retired principal with almost 40 years' teaching experience, "very few parents regret sending their child to school too late but many more regret sending children who were too young". Chapter 4 looks at early childhood development and provides some guidance on how to know if your child is "ready" for school. Ultimately, though, parents know their own children best and should rely on their own instincts.

Chapter 4

CHILD DEVELOPMENT DURING PRIMARY SCHOOL

Suzanne Guerin **and** *Gemma Kiernan*

INTRODUCTION

Starting primary school is a major transition in the lives of both young children and their families. With the growing use of child-care by Irish families, children are more likely to have had some contact with early childhood care and education settings, but the move to statutory primary education is still an important step. Children have to be able to make sense of new things in their environment, including different people and places. Parents need to consider issues around their child's age and development and how this will affect their readiness for school. In light of this, the aim of this chapter is to consider the child's development as they enter school and some of the related issues that may affect school selection and readiness. It should be noted, however, that this chapter will focus primarily on typically developing children, with some reference to potential challenges that children may encounter, such as learning difficulties and bullying. Other chapters in this book will provide parents will more in-depth information on these issues. This chapter will explore the role of the parent in this process and also provide parents with practical guidance, which will help them support and assess their child's progress through primary school.

THE DEVELOPMENTAL CONTEXT

The National Children's Strategy (Department of Health and Children, 2000), which was designed to provide a vision for children's lives in Ireland, places an emphasis on understanding the child as a whole. This means that it is important to understand the interactions between children's physical, emotional, social and cognitive (thinking and learning) development. As children prepare to enter school, there are a number of milestones that they reach around this time. However, it is important to note that these are simply guidelines and that children follow their own individual path of development. As a result, differences will occur in the age at which these milestones are reached.

Between the ages of four and six years, typically developing children acquire a number of abilities, characteristics and behaviours.

- During this time, children continue to develop physically, as seen in further changes in their *motor development*. This includes becoming more confident in activities such as running and jumping, and walking up and down stairs. While children may be less able and confident in their fine motor movements, such as picking up small objects and using crayons, etc. these also continue to develop.

- *Language development* also occurs. By the age of four, the child has a well-developed vocabulary and during this period children refine their speech further. For example, a child will ask direct questions, may talk about imaginary situations and will use concepts of time when talking to others.

- Another area of change relates to children's understanding of right and wrong (*moral development*). Marion Dowling (1995) describes how children begin to learn about rules during this time, particularly learning about the difference between social rules (putting your hand up in the classroom to ask a question) and moral rules (calling people nasty names).

- In terms of *social development*, children's ideas about friends are also changing and Noirin Hayes (1999) describes how, at this time, friends are seen as people to play with. She also comments on the way in which friendships can be broken by simple factors such as lack of contact or minor conflict.

- An important aspect of children's ability that is believed to develop during this phase is their understanding of other people's ideas and beliefs. This is called *theory of mind* (Harris, 1989). As this ability develops, children learn that the people around them do not see things in the same way as they do. This represents the beginning of perspective taking.

- A final area of development during this time relates to children's *understanding of gender*. It is generally agreed that by the age of six children understand that gender does not change based on clothes, hair length, etc.

This list refers to some of the major developmental changes that are thought to occur between the ages of four and six years. As was mentioned earlier, it is important that parents realise that not all children develop these abilities at the same time, and individual children will differ. However, if you are concerned about your child's development, do talk to their teacher as a child may display skills in school that parents may not see at home.

DEVELOPMENTAL ASPECTS OF SCHOOL READINESS

The previous section considered the development of children between four and six years. It is during this time that parents will be considering whether their child is ready for school. In Ireland, the legal requirement is that by six years, children should be in primary school. However, almost all five-year-olds and over half of all four-year-olds are enrolled in school (Department of Education and Science, 2003). When a child is ready to start school is a ques-

tion that has been debated by parents, practitioners and researchers at national and international level. For example, the Starting
School Research Project in Australia (Perry, Dockett and Howard,
2000; see http://golum.riv.csu.edu.au/~dopfer/s_school/index.htm
for further information) has gathered feedback from thousands of
parents, teachers and children on the issue of school readiness.

While definitions of readiness and ways of assessing it vary,
the body of knowledge in this area suggests that there are a number of key issues at play. While *age* is an obvious way of deciding
when children *should* go to school, there is a lack of conclusive
evidence concerning the benefits of starting school early, or starting school later. The best available evidence suggests that an early
introduction to a formal curriculum gives children an initial academic advantage, but that this advantage is not necessarily sustained in the longer term. Indeed, there are some suggestions that
an early introduction to a formal curriculum may increase anxiety
and have a negative impact on children's self-esteem and motivation to learn (see, for example, work done by Sylva and Nabuco,
1996). The evidence also suggests that there is no lasting advantage or disadvantage to children who enter school a year later
than their peer group. In drawing together the evidence from US
research on the impact of parents holding their children back from
starting school, Lilian Katz (2000) concluded that it was unclear
whether holding back is advantageous to children. Katz found
some evidence that children gain an academic and social advantage by being the oldest in the class, at least for the first three
years at school. On the other hand, there was evidence that, in the
longer term, "held back" children showed more behavioural
problems and used special education services more often than
their classmates. Rather than focusing just on age, it is more appropriate to consider when children are *ready* to go. There is a
range of other factors that may affect your child's readiness.

- Children's *physical health* is very important and a child who is
  healthy and well nourished will have the energy needed for a
  day at school. However, children who have been ill or have

special health needs may need additional support, such as breaks during the day or even shorter school days.

- Children's *mastery of particular school-related skills and knowledge* is often considered necessary for starting school and parents may emphasise skills such as being able to write your name or being able to count to 20. However, one of the interesting findings from the Australian Starting School project mentioned earlier is that teachers believe that these skills are not necessary because they can teach these things in school (Dockett and Perry, 2002). Indeed, some educators argue that it is more important that children show curiosity and enthusiasm for new activities.

- Another factor is *emotional readiness*. Children should feel positive about going to school and that they are happy in school. While some children may initially be upset or anxious at the beginning of the school day, this eventually disappears and the section on tips and resources for parents later in this chapter will suggest ways of helping your child to settle.

- Finally, your child's *social and communication skills* will play a role in their readiness for school. As mentioned earlier, children starting school will come into contact with many new people including other children, teachers and other adults. Children need to be capable of interacting with new people and forming relationships with them. This is particularly true of forming friendships. In order to do this, children need to be able to communicate their own thoughts and feelings and understand the thoughts and feelings of others.

The points above have considered the skills and abilities that may indicate your child's readiness for school. However, in addition to children being ready, schools also recognise the importance of being prepared to meet children's needs. Many schools have strategies to welcome and integrate children into school — for example, open days, individual pre-entry visits and parents being allowed to stay with their child for a time. The primary school curriculum gives teachers and schools the flexibility to respond to children at different levels of readiness.

FACTORS INVOLVED IN SCHOOL SELECTION

The Constitution of Ireland acknowledges the role of parents in the education of their children. Parents have choices in relation to the type of school they send their child to. At primary level, parents now have a wide choice of school types (see Chapter 5). In addition to making this choice, parents also have to consider factors such as the location of the school, whether the school is a single sex or mixed school, whether it is large or small, classroom size, and the cultural ethos of the school.

- *Location* is a very practical consideration when choosing a school for your child. Many parents show a preference for schools close to their home because they are the most convenient to access and require the least amount of travel time. While there are definite benefits to a school close by, if this is a priority you may find your choice of school is restricted to one school since that may be all that is available in your area.

- Parents are often divided on the issue of *single-sex versus mixed-sex schools*. Advocates of single-sex schooling claim that when girls are educated separately they learn in a less challenging environment and when boys are educated separately, they may be in a more active environment. Those who advocate mixed schools tend to see it as a healthier, more natural option, believing that boys and girls draw on each others' strengths and develop a better understanding of each other. Research examining the benefits of single-sex versus mixed schooling has generally focused on older children rather than children starting school and it has yielded mixed findings. Some studies have showed that both girls and boys benefited from studying in single-sex schools, while others have showed that while girls do better at single-sex schools, boys do better in mixed schools. Indeed, it has been observed that girls are often disadvantaged in co-educational schools because they have less opportunity to engage in questioning and discussion, whereas boys are asked for more information and are challenged more often. While the debate surrounding the advantages of single-sex versus mixed schools continues, research has demonstrated that mixed schools are associated with numerous personal and social benefits for children, including improved self-confidence and a better ability to make new friends.

- In considering *school size*, it is useful to be aware of the fact that children coming straight from home or from preschools in small self-contained buildings may be overwhelmed by the scale of school buildings. Children need to gain confidence in this new environment but rather than the size of the school, what is likely to be even more significant is the way in which children are introduced to their new environment. It appears from the evidence that children may find their new school easier to settle into if the child's initial transition into that setting is in the company of one or more people from a previous setting, for example, going to school with a friend or having an older sibling in the school.

- Aside from school size, a factor which may be more important is *teacher/child ratio and class size*. In Ireland, official teacher/child ratios are one teacher to a maximum of 29 children. However, recent figures from the Department of Education and Science show that some schools have higher ratios, while others have lower ratios. Teacher/child ratios are a central factor that impact on the quality of children's early educational experiences, with lower ratios typically being more favourable. In the US, for example, the National Association for the Education of Young Children recommends a ratio of ten children per staff member for four-year olds. While Irish infant classrooms do not meet this criterion, smaller class sizes are optimal in terms of children's experiences and academic achievement. There is broad agreement from research that smaller class sizes enable teachers to provide better quality education because they allow for more time for individualised and responsive teacher attention and interactions. In fact, the Department of Education and Science recognises the importance of lower ratios and several of their programmes, which have been designed to tackle educational disadvantage, have set ratios. For example, the *Breaking the Cycle* scheme (Department of Education, 1997) suggests a ratio of 15 children to one teacher in the infant classes. However, in reality many schools struggle to maintain low staff–pupil ratios due to limited resources at local and national level.

- Finally, the *cultural ethos* of the school warrants consideration. Irish society is becoming increasingly culturally diverse, a fact that is now recognised in government policy. The National Children's Strategy (2000) states that children should be educated and supported to value social and cultural diversity so that all children, including Travellers and other minority groups, achieve their full potential. In choosing a school, it may be useful to consider whether it caters respectfully for children's cultural background. For example, the school's religious ethos may be an important issue. Many Irish primary schools are under the management of one denomination or another and the majority of these are Roman Catholic. There is however, a growing choice of schools of other denominations and of multi-denominational schools. Schools that cater for a single religion may give priority to children of that religion but they will also admit children with other beliefs. Children do not have to attend religion class and parents may choose to withdraw their child from such classes if they wish. Another area to consider may be the role of the Irish language in a school. The Irish language is a part of many children's cultural heritage and is an integral aspect of the Irish education system. Children can learn Irish as part of the curriculum in primary school, but there is also evidence of growing interest among parents in having their children educated through Irish. For a more detailed consideration of these issues please see Chapter 5.

Consideration of the factors above can help parents make an informed choice about what school they consider will suit both them and their children best. Parents should also be aware of the benefits of speaking with parents of children who are already attending the school. These parents will be able to share their experiences in a particular school and this can be a very useful resource.

THE PARENTS' ROLE

As a child enters the busy school environment, it is essential to remember the key role parents continue to play in their child's adjustment during this change and in relation to their development in general. There is a large body of evidence which discusses the nature and importance of the child–parent attachment relationship. The attachment relationship has been shown to be important for both their survival and the quality of their development. Mary Ainsworth identified a number of types of attachment, the most common being "secure" attachments. Parents who are sensitive to their children, who respond consistently to them and who provide warmth and care, encourage the formation of a secure attachment. The security or this attachment may be compromised by stress and conflict within the family. One of the areas of debate in relation to attachment is whether it is more beneficial for children to be cared for by parents or childcare professionals. It has been suggested that childcare has a negative impact on this bond; however, there is evidence to suggest that not only can children benefit from good quality day care, but that the parent–child relationship can also be enhanced by daily separation. This is a topic that continues to generate debate and Hayes (1999) considers this issue in more detail.

More relevant to the topic at hand is the contribution of this attachment relationship to the child's experience on entering school. Children who have secure attachments adjust better to school, as they are more able to cope with unfamiliar environments and people, as they are confident that their parent will return for them at the end of the day. However, children experiencing difficulties in this area may be more anxious and distressed at the idea of separation from their parent.

Moving beyond the attachment relationship, Margaret Henry, in her book, *Young Children, Parents and Professionals* (1996), considers the multiple roles that parents have during this time. These include learning about their child's development, supporting their development, and importantly making decisions about their child's education. However, one central point that Henry makes is that parents fill these roles in conjunction with professionals such as teachers. Henry describes this aspect as a "partnership". She goes on to talk about how teachers and parents can support each other by sharing information about the child, a process that can only benefit the child's experience.

Another important role parents can play in their child's development as they move into and adjust to this new environment is to listen to them and in many ways represent their views when necessary. In recent years, there has been a growing emphasis on the importance of listening to children. Evidence of this can be seen in the UN Convention on the Rights of the Child (United Nations, 1989) and in the National Children's Strategy (Department of Health and Children, 2000). Many researchers and practitioners have considered the value of consulting children on a wide range of issues, including bullying in school (Guerin and Hennessy, 2002), children's experiences in care (Oakley, 2000) and children's perspectives on separation (Hogan, Halpanney and Green, 2002).

While many of these studies have focused on the views of slightly older children, there is evidence that children as young as four can be asked for their views and experiences. In fact, the Starting School Project in Australia, mentioned earlier, has talked with children between four and six years about their experiences of starting school. Sue Dockett and Bob Perry (1999) argue that it is essential to listen to the views of children, as well as those of parents, at this time and that they can contribute a valuable insight. For example, when they were asked what children needed to know when they are starting school, the most common response was rules. The children talked about what was termed "conventional rules", which included rules around school routine such as sitting in your place, listening to the teacher, and good behaviour. A second common response related to children's attitudes to and feelings about school (called dispositions). In discussing these dispositions, children talked about positive and negative feelings about school including being excited and happy, or alternatively being sad and scared. This particular point is important as it supports the idea that young children are able to talk about how going to school makes them feel, and what areas might be problematic for them. The later section, "Tips and Resources for Parents", outlines some things to keep in mind when talking to a child about going to school.

ASSESSING A CHILD'S PROGRESS

When children start school, parents are not only concerned that their child settles in well, but that they also make good progress. While some parents may have concerns around the idea of assessing young children, it is important to remember that assessment has a valuable role to play in children's development. It is only by assessing children's progress that parents and teachers can effectively support their development and encourage their learning. The obvious question then is, how can parents assess their child's progress and learning in infant classes? There are several important things to keep in mind when trying to assess a child's learning. These include what to look for and how to look for it.

- *What to look for?* Often learning is evaluated from the perspective of what children *cannot* do. While this is important, particularly if children are experiencing developmental delays or difficulties, it is more meaningful to consider what children *can* do. With this in mind, parents also need to remember that children are developing across many domains during the early school years, and that it is necessary to consider their development and learning in all these areas, including the academic, social and emotional domains.

- *How to look for it?* Assessing a child's learning in school is generally a very simple process of observing, understanding, and acting (Drummond, 1993). Observation involves following a child's progress by watching what they can do (for example, if they bring artwork home from school), talking to and listening to them about what they have learned in class and also talking with the teacher about their progress. Understanding involves reflecting on the information gathered on a child's progress but also placing this in context. This may involve being aware of the typical path of child development (keeping in mind the natural variation in development) and a child's progress in relation to this. However, it may also involve looking at a child's development across different domains. For example a parent may be concerned that their child is doing very well in some areas but not in others. The final aspect of assessing progress is acting on both observations and understanding. In the situation above, a parent may decide, in consultation with the teacher, that this is not a cause for concern, or there may be a need for a course of action. This can come in many forms, ranging from additional parental support and guidance to professional advice and input.

- *Communication:* In considering a child's progress, learning and development, communication between parents and teachers is vital. Parents play a key role in understanding progress because they have a wealth of information about their own children. Equally, teachers can share insights with parents on their child's learning and development. This two-way communication helps to ensure consistency in learning as the child moves between their home and school environments. As mentioned in earlier sections, this sharing of information (e.g. when dropping children off at school/picking them up, at parent–teacher meetings) strengthens the partnership between the teacher and the parents, and ultimately benefits the child.

In summary, being aware of their child's progress can help parents ensure that they continue to develop appropriately, that any potential difficulties are identified early, and that these difficulties can be addressed.

FACTORS AFFECTING A CHILD'S SCHOOL EXPERIENCE

There are a multitude of factors that can negatively affect a child's experience in school, including both internal and external forces. Two of the most common concerns for parents are learning difficulties and problematic social interactions.

In recent years parents and educators have become increasingly aware of the challenge of learning difficulties. However, it is important to recognise that there are a broad range of factors that can affect a child's ability to learn. Learning difficulties are most often associated with disabilities or diagnosed impairments (see Chapter 7), but other factors such as diet and sleep patterns can affect the child's ability to learn in the classroom. For example, there is powerful research evidence to support the link between a nutritious breakfast and improved concentration, mood and academic performance. This link is not limited to a good breakfast and highlights the need for a well-balanced diet. Another possible area of concern is language and again children can experience difficulties in this area due to both specific disabilities and more complex environmental factors. These problems can include limited vocabulary and a tendency to avoid communicating with others.

In terms of problematic social interactions, the most obvious issue that parents will be concerned about is bullying. Bullying is a common problem in schools; however, most children experience minor difficulties in this area. Serious and persistent bullying, while upsetting and challenging, is rare. In Chapter 10 some of these issues are considered in more detail; however, it is important to address possible responses to these problems at this point.

How will parents know if their child is experiencing any of these difficulties? There are many "signs" that have been suggested to indicate that children are experiencing problems, including a sudden reluctance to go to school, changes in mood and behaviour patterns (including sleeping and eating) and the occurrence of bedwetting. However, parents should be aware that children may not show any obvious signs of difficulty and therefore they need to be confident in their ability to identify problems by alternative means. The first of these is knowledge of their child's typical demeanour. Parents need to be sensitive to changes in their child's behaviour, which may indicate a problem. This can involve observing your child in the different environment they are in, i.e. school, home and playtime. This observation can allow parents to identify possible sources of these changes, however observation by itself is often not enough. The second means of identifying problems is to talk to the child directly (and this is considered in the "Tips and Resources" section of this chapter) and explore what, if anything they are concerned about or having problems with. Thirdly, parents may find it helpful to talk with other adults the child may spend time with. This may include teachers, childminders and other adult family members to see if they have noticed any changes or are aware of any problems. The "Tips and Resources" section again provides information on approaching your child's teacher.

Finally, it is possible that even after following these steps parents may still be concerned about their child's wellbeing. In such cases, parents should seek the advise of professionals including their GP and local health clinic.

CHILD DEVELOPMENT DURING PRIMARY SCHOOL

Having considered all the factors involved in selecting a school, and tackling the possible challenges a child may face as they adjust to the school environment, parents may be interested in what lies ahead for their child in terms of their development over the course of their time in primary school. Just as this chapter started by considering the developmental milestones a child is likely to have reached as they start school, this section considers the major developmental milestones he or she is likely to achieve during their primary school years. This period is often referred to as *middle childhood* (six to twelve years).

- Children continue to develop physically during middle childhood, with increases in height and weight as well as in speed and strength. *Motor skills* continue to develop, including fine motor co-ordination (which is involved in writing).

- *Language development* also continues, with huge increases in children's vocabulary. Their understanding and use of grammar also improves. Related skills include the development of literacy, which show rapid changes during this period.

- The child's ability to make sense of information (*cognitive development*) continues to develop and there are improvements in their ability to think about problems in a logical way. These developments allow children to begin to understand mathematical concepts like addition, subtraction, etc. Related skills include improved memory and attention.

- Children's understanding of rules (*moral development*) continues to develop. For example, children now realise that rules are not necessarily fixed and that groups can agree to change them. In the later part of this period, another important skill is the realisation that they will not get punished for breaking a rule unless they are caught.

- In terms of *social development*, one of the major changes is the growing importance of friends and friendships. Later in middle childhood, children see close friends as people they can rely on and trust, and as such, they will be influenced by their friends in many ways. However, the parent continues to play an important role, providing the child with a secure base from which to explore and develop new relationships.

- One interesting aspect of friendships relates to *gender*. During this period children tend to show a preference for same-sex friendships — boys will play with boys, and girls will play with girls. While gender is important in friendships at this time, other qualities continue to play a role in children's choice of friends.

Again, as was mentioned earlier, children's paths of development will vary and not all children develop at the same rate. However, middle childhood continues to be an exciting period of change in children's lives.

TIPS AND RESOURCES FOR PARENTS

The final section of this chapter offers simple tips and suggestions for parents to help their child to settle into and thrive in school.

Knowing Your Child is Ready for School

- *Communication*: Your child should be able to understand others and to be understood.

- *Learning skills*: Your child should be able to concentrate on a simple task, and to pay attention to people around them.

- *Physical skills*: Your child should have some dressing skills and be able to use the bathroom. They should also be comfortable with fine motor skills like holding a pencil or crayon.

- *Social skills*: Your child should be able to play with and, importantly, share with others. Also, it is important that your child can respond to instructions or correction by the teacher.

- *Emotional skills*: It is helpful if your child is comfortable being away from you for relatively short periods of time. If a child is confident that their parent will return they are more likely to settle in a new environment.

Helping Your Child Adjust to School

In helping your child to adjust, it is beneficial if parents have a positive and relaxed attitude towards school. Some key things to remember include:

- Visit the school with your child before the first day. As mentioned earlier, many schools have scheduled open days to facilitate this.

- Involve your child in preparations like buying uniforms, etc. Let them help pick out things like school bags, pencil cases and lunchboxes.

- Talk with your child about what they are looking forward to about school and what worries they may have, and try to answer any questions they have.

- Parents should try to take their child to school for the first few days of school. Alternatively, arrange for a familiar person to do it so that the child has a link to their home environment.

- Going with friends or an older brother or sister (if there is one) can also help.

- Familiarise yourself with school policies, for example those relating to uniforms, lunches and discipline. This will aid your understanding of the guidelines that influence your child's school day.

How to Talk to Your Child about School

As was mentioned above, talking to your child about school can help them to adjust. This continues to be important throughout their school lives.

- Talk with your child regularly about school. While this is important in itself, it also means that if a problem arises your child is used to talking about school matters.

- Remember to listen to what your child tells you. All parents lead busy lives, and sometimes it is easy to be distracted when your child is talking to you.

- Find an appropriate time and place to talk to your child. This should not be a formal time, but can be at mealtimes when the family is discussing their day, when a child has brought an art project home from school, or even on the way home from school.

- Always ask your child about their experiences in school in a casual and relaxed way. This can be difficult, particularly if you are worried about a problem or incident. Remember, the way you react to your child in this type of situation may affect whether they will come to you with their concerns again.

- However, while it is important to be relaxed, never dismiss concerns that your child may share.

How to Approach Your Child's School

Parents have many reasons to contact their child's school, ranging from getting information on school events to dealing with possible difficulties. Teachers and school staff are always willing to speak with parents, but keeping a few things in mind can help the process.

- While teachers are always willing to speak with parents, it is important to remember to find the right time to do this. The start of the school day can be very busy, so try to arrange a good time with the teacher.

- Be sure to attend any parent–teacher meetings the school organises. This gives both parents and teachers a chance to talk about a child's progress.

- If you do need to talk with the teacher about a problem your child is having remember to be calm and to communicate your concerns clearly. Listen to what the teacher has to say and work together to find the best way to tackle the problem.

- Attending school events, such as sports days and Christmas concerts, can also be very important. Not only do children enjoy the chance to share their achievements with their parents, but these events also provide the parents with a useful means of strengthening their relationship with their child's teacher, as well as getting to know other staff including teachers your child may have in the future and the school principal.

CONCLUSION

Many factors influence children's growth and development. School is a particularly influential part of both children's lives and their development and learning. Therefore, the transition to school and the decisions involved need to be given careful consideration. Equally important is ensuring that school is a positive experience for a child. This chapter has outlined some of the major developmental changes associated with the school years in order to provide a context for a child's experience. It has also highlighted the vital role of the parents in supporting development and learning during this time. By understanding the issues and challenges involved, parents are in a better position to ensure that their child's school years are fulfilling and beneficial.

References

Department of Education (1997), *Breaking the Cycle*, Information Leaflet, Dublin: The Stationery Office.

Department of Education and Science (1999), *Primary School Curriculum: Your Child's Learning — Guidelines for Parents*, Dublin: The Stationery Office.

Department of Education and Science (2003), *Statistical Report 2001–2002*, Dublin: The Stationery Office.

Department of Health and Children (2000), *The National Children's Strategy. Our Children — Their Lives*, Dublin: The Stationery Office.

Dockett, S. and Perry, B. (1999), "Starting School: What Do the Children Say?" *Early Child Development and Care*, 159, 107–119.

Dockett, S. and Perry, B. (2002), "Who's Ready for What? Young Children Starting School", *Contemporary Issues in Early Childhood*, 3(1), 67–89.

Dowling, M. (1995), *Starting School at Four: A Joint Endeavour*, London: Paul Chapman Publishing.

Drummond, M.J. (1993), *Assessing Children's Learning*, London: David Fulton Publishers.

Guerin, S. and Hennessy, E. (2002), *Aggression and Bullying*, Parent, Adolescent and Child Training Skills (PACTS) Series, Oxford: BPS Blackwell.

Harris, P.L. (1989), *Children and Emotion: The Development of Psychological Understanding*, Oxford: Blackwell Publishers.

Hayes, N. (1999), *Early Childhood: An Introductory Text (2nd Edition)*, Dublin: Gill and Macmillan.

Henry, M. (1996), *Young Children, Parents and Professionals*, London; Routledge.

Hogan, D.M., Halpanney, A.M. and Green, S. (2002), *Children's Experience of Parental Separation*, Dublin: Children's Research Centre, Trinity College.

Katz, L.G. (2000), *Academic Redshirting and Young Children*, Document available online at http://npin.org/library/2001/n00520.n00520.html.

Oakley, M.W., (2000), "Children and Young People and Care Proceedings", in A. Lewis and G. Lindsay (Eds.), *Researching Children's Perspectives*, pp. 73–85, Buckingham: Open University Press.

Perry, B., Dockett, S. and Howard, P. (2000), "Starting School: Issues for Children, Parents and Teachers", *Journal of Australian Research in Early Childhood Education*, 7(1), 41–53.

Sylva, K. and Nabuco, M. (1996), "Research on Quality in the Curriculum", *International Journal of Early Childhood*, 28(2), 1–6.

Chapter 5

TYPES OF SCHOOLS

COMPARING SCHOOL TYPES

As previously mentioned in Chapter 1, schools in Ireland fall into two classes: recognised and unrecognised. These schools are further divided, at the primary level, into a number of categories according to ownership and ethos, as will be discussed later in the chapter.

If you read most school brochures or literature there is a high probability that it will mention that it strives to provide a child-centred, caring environment, where a holistic approach to education is taken and concern is given to the development of the whole of the child's abilities as well as their academic attainments. They will often mention that all pupils are treated equally and that bullying is not tolerated. All of these well-meaning schools may well be living up to the aspirations outlined in their prospectuses; however, the challenge for parents is to determine how closely the ideals are translated into practical policies and daily experiences.

It is probably useful to begin any comparisons between school types by mentioning the factors that they have in common alongside those that distinguish them from each other. These factors are discussed below under the following headings:

- Legislation and guidelines

- Management

- Curriculum

- Teacher training and qualifications

- Resources

- Ethos.

Legislation and Guidelines

All schools are now required to operate under the provisions of the Education Act 1998 and the Education (Welfare) Act 2000. As has been explained in Chapter 1 these Acts set out to provide a statutory basis for the delivery of education, something that had not previously existed. In the past, the independent schools, in so far as they were unaided by public funds, were largely free to set out their own policies. However, as is explained in Chapter 8, since the introduction of the Education (Welfare) Act 2000 all pupils (regardless of sector) will be required to be registered, and the National Educational Welfare Board must assess and monitor the standard of education provided by these schools and be satisfied that pupils are receiving an appropriate minimum education.

Management

The management of recognised schools is overseen by the board of management, whose function has already been outlined in Chapter 1. This ensures consistency and a degree of public scrutiny and accountability in publicly funded schools. The governing associations for each school sector provide training to boards in the execution of their duties as well as guidelines, advice and backup. There are a variety of management structures in independent schools from boards of trustees to single owner/ managers or principals with direction from a religious superior.

Obviously the quality of management in any organisation largely determines how it functions. There is extensive research to support the theory that where there is an experienced management in place with effective leadership and a clear and cohesive unity of purpose, the outcome is an improvement in the teaching and learning environment. There are more likely to be differences between schools from the same sector as between sectors in term of quality of management.

Recognised schools are subject to inspection by the Department of Education inspectors. Inspectors visit schools to evaluate their organisation and operation and the quality and effectiveness of the education provided, including the quality of teaching and effectiveness of individual teachers. The inspection system has been described in Chapter 1.

Curriculum

Due to the widespread approval for the 1999 Primary School Curriculum, all schools (including those in the independent sector) use it as the basis for planning and implementing the educational experience. Some schools have been more efficient in implementing the new curriculum than others and the level of co-ordination right through the grades will have an impact on the outcomes for pupils. The 1999 curriculum is described in more detail in Chapter 6.

Teacher Training and Qualifications

Teachers qualified to teach in the primary school system must have a Bachelor in Education Degree (B.Ed.). The B.Ed. is a three-year course and there are specified minimum requirements in Irish, English and Maths. Entry is through the CAO application system and based on statistics for 2004, a candidate would require an average of grade B3 in six subjects.

There are five recognised colleges for the training and education of teachers:

- Church of Ireland College of Education, Upper Rathmines Rd., Dublin
- Froebel College, Sion Hill, Blackrock, County Dublin
- Mary Immaculate College of Education, Limerick
- St Mary's College of Education, Griffith Ave., Marino, Dublin
- St Patrick's College, Drumcondra, Dublin.

There is also a system for taking mature students and a graduate training scheme to allow graduates to undergo a year-long course after which they would be recognised as primary teachers.

There are a number of restrictions to the employment of teachers who have been trained outside the state but they can be employed on a provisional basis while they are preparing for the Scrúdú Cáilíochta sa Ghaeilge (SCG), which is essential for teaching Irish. Montessori-trained teachers are not recognised fully for primary teaching but can be employed in some special classes and special schools.

Hibernia College in Dublin also runs an online post-graduate teacher-training course, which is approved by HETAC (Higher Education and Training Awards Council) and the Department of Education. The course includes a minimum of 14 weeks' teaching practice and a course of study in the Irish language, including on-site lectures in the Gaeltacht. It lasts 18 months.

Due to a shortage in the past number of years not all schools have been able to recruit fully qualified teachers. The Irish National Teachers Organisation advises that there are approximately 600 people in the service who do not hold a recognised teaching qualification. In addition there are hundreds of people employed as substitutes who cover for short-term absences, most of whom are not qualified.

Due to the fact that staff in independent schools are not paid by the state, there is more flexibility in the levels of qualifications that they will accept. While there are many highly qualified teachers in that sector it is worth asking as in all schools what the level of qualification is.

Resources

The Department of Education funds the day-to-day running costs of schools in addition to providing funds for curriculum areas (e.g. PE equipment, science material, money for books, computers). However, most schools still have a shortfall. School boards are obliged to ask for voluntary donations to cope with the shortfall. In disadvantaged areas and in smaller schools the funding that can be raised in this way is obviously limited and therefore they will be restricted in what they can provide. Well-established and larger schools will have the benefit of scale. Some schools will have the benefit of a non-teaching principal and in some cases a full-time secretary and caretaker. In the independent sector there is also a wide range of resources available depending on the size, age and type of school.

Ethos

The Education Act 1998 refers to the characteristic spirit of the school as "determined by the cultural, educational, moral, religious, social, linguistic and spiritual values and traditions which inform and are characteristic of the objectives and conduct of the school" (see Chapter 2). This broad definition attempts to explain what can be a fairly nebulous yet essential categorisation. In some way this provides the core differences between schools, especially in the case of denominational schools. Those who have very clear preferences with regard to the ethos of their ideal school in some ways have an easier decision. For those whose over-riding criterion is a "good" school, regardless of whether it is denominational, multi-denominational, gaelscoil or independent, the choice can be more difficult.

OVERVIEW OF SCHOOL TYPES

In our research for this book, we invited the national governing bodies of each organisation to submit a brief description of their sector, explaining the features of the educational environment that they had to offer. The remainder of this chapter is largely adapted and edited from their descriptions. The views expressed in the remainder of this chapter are therefore those of the representative organisations, and do not reflect either the views of the editors, of individual schools, staff or parents. The school types are discussed below under the following headings:

- Catholic Primary Schools

- Protestant Primary Schools

- Gaelscoileanna

- Educate Together Schools

- Private or Independent Schools

- Special Schools.

There are also two Muslim schools under the patronage of the Islamic Foundation of Ireland; and there is one Jewish/multi-denominational school in Dublin. Finally, there are two French schools and a German school in Dublin.

Catholic Primary Schools[1]

School Structure

About 96 per cent of all primary schools are under the patronage of the Catholic Church and are privately owned by the religious orders or by the Church. The patron of all Catholic schools is the local bishop. The bishop appoints a board of management to manage the school on his behalf in accordance with the Education Act 1998. The patron nominates trustees of the school to be parties to the lease of the school and to the deed of variation. The Catholic primary school is a parish school and its enrolment policy gives priority to the Catholic children of the parish.

Boards of management of Catholic primary schools are members of the Catholic Primary School Management Association (CPSMA). Each diocese sends six delegates to an Annual Provincial Council meeting. The AGM of CPSMA takes place in the spring of each year. Each diocese sends six delegates to the AGM. A Standing Committee is elected every four years at the AGM. The Standing Committee negotiates with the DES and the other education partners on all issues pertaining to Catholic primary education.

---

[1] This overview was submitted by Fr Dan O'Connor of the Catholic Primary School Management Association (CPSMA).

The board of management is the employer of the school staff and the board must be aware and adhere to the employment and equality legislation. Catholic schools are obliged to follow the rules for national schools, the provision of the circulars issued by the Minister and the constitution and rules of procedure.

Parents and Pupils

The Catholic school exists for the pupils. The enrolment policy of a Catholic school gives priority to the Catholic children of the parish and to the sisters and brothers of children already enrolled in the school (in accordance with EU regulations siblings have a right to be educated together). Catholic schools not only in Ireland and in Europe but throughout the world have always been places where people of other faiths and no faith are welcome. There are excellent examples of good practice of the way Catholic primary schools provide for students of other faiths without watering down or changing the ethos of a school. The primary school is a parish school for the Catholic pupils but once a school has provided for the Catholic pupils the school Board is obliged to accept all who apply for the other vacant places in a school. The Church's teaching acknowledges that the parents are the primary educators of their children, as does the Irish Constitution. The Catholic school strives to make parents feel welcome in the school.

Religious Instruction, Formation and Ethos

In 1997 an agreed wording between all the partners in Catholic primary schools — i.e. National Parents Council (Primary), INTO, CPSMA, the Catholic bishops and the Minister for Education — resulted in the "Schedule for a Catholic School":

> A Roman Catholic School (which is established in connection with the Minister) aims at promoting the full and harmonious development of all aspects of the person of the pupil: intellectual, physical, cultural, moral and spiritual, including a living relationship with God and with other people. The school models and promotes a philosophy of life inspired by belief in God and in the life, death and resurrection of Jesus

Christ. The Catholic school provides Religious Education for
the pupils in accordance with the doctrines, practices and
tradition of the Roman Catholic Church and promotes the
formation of the pupils in the Catholic Faith.

This schedule places a serious responsibility on the boards and
schools under Catholic patronage. The ethos of a Catholic school
— or, as described in the Education Act, "the characteristic spirit"
— is based on not only providing religious instruction and formation of the pupils in the faith, and preparing the students for the
sacraments but also on other elements, including the celebration
of the Eucharist in school; prayer life in the school; religious symbols in each classroom; the provision of a Bible and Religious
Education materials for each classroom; the role of the priest as
chaplain to the students, parents and staff; the involvement of the
parents in the religious education, instruction and formation of
the pupils in the faith not only at sacramental time but throughout
the pupils' time in primary and post-primary education.

Under Rule 68 for national schools, religious instruction is
provided in denominational schools. However, Catholic primary
schools must make provision for pupils whose parents do not
wish them to attend religious instruction. Rule 69 applies to the
rights of parents and pupils as follows:

2(a) No pupil shall receive, or be present at, any religious
instruction of which parents or guardian disapprove.

(b) The periods of formal religious instruction shall be fixed
so as to facilitate the withdrawal of pupils to whom
paragraph (a) of this section applies.

3   Where such religious instruction as their parents or
guardians approve is not provided in the school for any
section of the pupils, such pupils must, should their
parents or guardians so desire, be allowed to absent
themselves from school, at reasonable times, for the
purpose of receiving that instruction elsewhere.

The school is required under the Education Act to provide for the
full formation of the pupil and a Catholic school strives for excel-

lence so that each pupil will benefit from the education provided and be able to achieve the fullness of their potential.

However, faith formation is not just a school-based activity but is based from the home, the parish and the school. The Catholic community must support and encourage parents in their central role. It is unfair and unjust to leave the total task to the teachers. True education involves co-operation and support of the home, the school and the parish.

The Catholic Primary School Management Association can be contacted at Veritas House, 7/8 Lower Abbey Street, Dublin 1; Tel: 01-8742171; E-mail: cpsma@indigo.ie.

Protestant Primary Schools[2]

School Structure

Those schools described as under the patronage of the Protestant Churches would more correctly be described as under the patronage of the Church of Ireland, Methodist Church of Ireland or the Presbyterian Church of Ireland, together with a number of schools which may be federal in patronage, representing partnership between two or three of those Churches. There are some 200 schools under the patronage of Protestant Churches including 16 Presbyterian and one Methodist school. Because the Protestant population is small and widely dispersed, the size of the schools is generally small in terms of individual enrolments; almost half of such schools have only two class teachers with a multi-grade group in each classroom.

The schools are owned by the Church and the patron is usually the local bishop. He will have an oversight role in ensuring that the characteristic spirit is upheld and in supporting the ongoing development of the school. Occasionally where certain school issues are unresolved the patron may provide an appeal mechanism.

---

[2] This overview was submitted by Canon John McCullagh of the Church of Ireland Board of Education.

The Church of Ireland Board of Education provides an advisory service to all boards of management, patrons and the school communities within the sector. It is able to do this as it maintains a full-time education officer. Contact details are listed on page 96.

Ethos or Characteristic Spirit

Protestant national schools are denominational in character, reflecting the tradition and teaching of the sponsoring Church, but the schools have a multi-denominational intake as they cater primarily for the entire Protestant community together with those who find the ethos amenable. The following may be helpful in understanding the ethos of such schools.

A Church of Ireland school is a community where all pupils are equally valued and respected — irrespective of gender, social background, family circumstances, education achievement, physical characteristics or intellectual functioning. Pupils experience a sense of caring and belonging, they are treated fairly and their spiritual, moral and religious development is encouraged as is their intellectual, social and academic development. The school community is one where moral values such as honesty, truthfulness, justice, fairness, sensitivity to others and civic responsibility are nurtured and protected. The justification of these qualities is based on biblical teaching interpreted by the appropriate sponsoring Church. The Church of Ireland primary school is part of the local church community who will have strong links with the parish. It is likely that pupils will attend assembly in the local church and that the rector will visit the school and conduct assemblies in the school itself.

While there is a very strong and clear church link, nonetheless the work of the school is conducted in an atmosphere of tolerance and respect for religious differences. The admission policy of such schools allows those of other faiths or none to become pupils provided that the existing ethos is respected.

There is an agreed Religious Education programme, *Follow Me*, which includes among its aims the enabling of children to develop a knowledge and understanding of beliefs, worship and witness of the Christian faith, to explore the biblical witness to God as Trinity and to develop an awareness of and sensitivity to those of other faiths and none. The foregoing does not in any way invalidate the right of parents to withdraw their children from religious education classes. The teaching of religious education takes place at specific timetabled periods using the timeframe approved by the NCCA but in common with the approach throughout the primary school curriculum there will be in many schools the opportunity for integration and for linking with other subject areas. The story of Noah may be portrayed in drama while preparation for the story may take place during visual arts periods. Likewise there will be strong links with SPHE.

A Church of Ireland school is one where the traditions and teachings of that Church will inform the position taken in regard to moral issues which arise in the teaching of curricular subjects. The school, however, nurtures freedom of thought and a personal relationship with God. This will be most evident in the teaching of religious education and in the prayer life of the school community. The preparation of children for specific church membership such as confirmation does not take place within school time but in the child's parish or congregation. The foregoing description might equally apply to a Methodist or Presbyterian school with very little change other than semantics.

Gaeilge is an essential element of the curriculum and is not merely the learning of the language but an exploration of culture and history. Pupils will learn about the contribution of individuals like Douglas Hyde and Erskine Childers to the development of our state.

Role of Parents

Parents play a key role both individually and collectively in terms of the development and support of the school and in drawing particular issues and concerns to the attention of the principal and board of management. Every parent should feel welcomed and be encouraged to be involved in the Parents' Association or PTA, depending upon which is available in your local school. Primary education should not involve a cost to parents but inevitably there will be fund-raising or a request for a family contribution towards the provision of equipment or services not covered by the normal government grants. Some schools are delighted to avail of voluntary assistance by parents in areas such as library, reading or sport.

It may seem curious when dealing with primary education but it is important to plan your child's transfer to second level within a short time of your child being enrolled in the infant class. This is particularly important in certain areas of Dublin and provincial cities where there may be considerable pressure on places.

It may also be necessary to avail of school transport; in fact, many schools in this sector avail of the Department's school transport scheme, which recognises the right of a parent to send their child to a (denominational) school of their choice.

The education officer of the Church of Ireland Board of Education may be contacted at Church of Ireland House, Church Avenue, Rathmines, Dublin 6; Tel: 01-4978422, E-mail: boe@rcbdub.org.

Gaelscoileanna[3]

School Structure

A gaelscoil is essentially a school where all subjects are taught through Irish except for English and other languages. Irish is the language of the school, between children, teachers and parents. A gaelscoil is an immersion school where students are totally immersed in Irish from the start of the day.

There are two kinds of gaelscoileanna. Gaelscoileanna in Gaeltacht areas are vested in the local diocese and are in fact identical to ordinary national schools and have the normal board of management, appointed by the local bishop, except that of course they deliver education through the medium of Irish.

Gaelscoileanna Teo, the body responsible for the promotion of these schools was founded by concerned parents and teachers in 1973 and is recognised by the Department of Education and

---

[3] This overview was submitted by Colm Ó Dulacháin of Gaelscoileanna Teo.

Science. The organisation is principally funded by Foras na Gaeilge. There are over 23,000 children attending 121 gaelscoileanna in the Republic outside of Gaeltacht areas. Prior to 1993, most of these schools were established under the patronage of the local Catholic bishop. In 1993, a group of parents in Mayfield in Cork wished that the religious ethos of their gaelscoil be multi-denominational. This led to the formation of Foras Pátrúnachta na Scoileanna LánGhaeilge, who now have 47 schools in the Republic under their patronage. Those establishing a gaelscoil at primary level have a choice of bodies that they can invite to be patron of the school. Parents setting up new schools can decide in consultation with An Foras Pátrúnachta whether the religious ethos be Catholic, interdenominational or multidenominational.

Gaelscoileanna Teo is a voluntary body with a Board of Directors of up to 20 members, composed of parents, members of boards of management and teachers. The Board of Directors is elected at the Annual Congress which is held in different venues around the country. The principal aim of Gaelscoileanna Teo is to develop Irish-medium education around the country and help schools provide the best possible education through the medium of Irish by helping gaelscoileanna at both levels to develop and grow and overcome problems or difficulties. The organisation assists parents who wish to establish Irish medium schools in their areas and they publish a comprehensive guidebook on how to set up a gaelscoil in your area. The organisation has a full-time permanent staff of five. Contact details are listed on page 99.

Ethos and Bilingualism

Many parents choose a primary-level gaelscoil because their children will learn Irish from a very early age. Because children learn through play, music and gestures when they start school they enjoy learning the language and are proud of being able to understand and speak it fluently at an early age. When children are in a natural language environment throughout the school day the language comes to them easily and naturally. They become bilingual quickly, which helps their own self-confidence and increases their respect for the language.

Linguists have cited other advantages which accrue from all-Irish education. They point to international research which shows that being bilingual helps intellectual and cognitive development. Children understand that words are merely a means of explaining different things. They realise that there is not a direct link between a word and an object and that there are different ways of describing things.

Some linguists assert that children who can speak two language can be more self-confident. They enjoy translating for their parents and helping them to form simple sentences. Simply put, they say that having two languages gives twice the choice.

Bilingualism opens windows on two cultures. Being bilingual from an early age makes it easier for children to learn a third or fourth language when they are older. They have experienced learning another language easily and understand that learning other languages is possible. It promotes greater tolerance and less racism, which is important as Ireland becomes more multicultural. Some of the character advantages of being bilingual, according to Colin Baker, Professor of Education at the University of Wales, are a heightened security in national and cultural identity and greater self-esteem.

Parents are invited to send their children to the gaelscoil at junior infants level. While they and their parents need not be proficient in Irish, it is important that parents support and encourage the child to speak Irish. Many gaelscoileanna have Irish language classes for parents so that they may bring the language from the classroom to the home. Parents who are concerned that they will have problems helping children with homework learn Irish for that reason. In reality, however, children whose two languages are well developed translate the tasks for their parents thereby letting the monolingual parent be involved in the process.

While over 24,000 pupils attend all-Irish primary schools, fewer than 6,000 attend second-level gaelscoileanna. The number of post-primary schools is increasing but a question arises for many parents about the potential difficulties in transferring from primary gaelscoileanna to English-language post-primary schools. Some parents are comfortable with their children learning through Irish in primary school but consider that at second level the child should concentrate on getting good examination results to go on to third-level colleges. This is a concern raised in many countries where the second language is a minority one. There is no reason, however, that children cannot switch languages from primary to second level. They are leaving a system that is a child-centred one and moving to a subject-driven one where the whole system changes.

The main office of Gaelscoileanna Teo is located at 7 Merrion Square, Dublin 2. Further information, including a list of primary and post-primary schools, can be found at www.gaelscoileanna.ie or by contacting the office at 01-6398431 or by E-mail at oifig@gaelscoileanna.ie.

Educate Together Schools[4]

School Structure

Educate Together schools are set up and developed by groups of parents in a local area who wish to send their children to a national school that is multi-denominational, child-centred, co-educational and democratically run. These four principles under-pin the daily life of each school as well as characterising the ethos of the organisation as a whole. Educate Together schools are fully recognised by the Department of Education and Science, are non-fee-paying and operate under the same rules that apply to all national schools. They cover the same curriculum as laid out by the Department and subscribe to the same state inspections as every other national school does.

While child-centredness has been the core concept of the National School Curriculum since 1971, and co-educational primary schools are now common, the democratic nature of Educate

---

[4] This overview was submitted by Deirdre Mangaoang of Educate Together.

Together is a unique feature in Irish primary education and generates considerable interest. Educate Together schools are originally set up by parents in their local area but parental involvement does not fade once the school opens its doors. Parents and members of the wider community are encouraged to get actively involved at every level, from organising extra-curricular school events, to serving on a board of management, to being elected as a director of Educate Together. The current board of directors is made up of ten elected members and two co-optees, all of whom have committed their time voluntarily to lead the organisation on the national stage. Throughout the sector this degree of voluntary parental involvement works in partnership with the professional role of teachers and principals, and is crucial to its success as a whole. Because they are so rooted in a living community, the schools can and do become important community resources making their facilities available in an appropriate way outside school hours.

Ethos

The question asked most frequently about Educate Together schools surrounds the concept of multi-denominational education. In Ireland these schools are a relatively new development and can be perceived to be in sharp contrast to the traditional primary education scene, which is dominated by religious influences. Put simply, Educate Together schools are obliged to respect the rights of each child, irrespective of the child's social, cultural or religious background. Each school organises a comprehensive programme of ethical education about different faiths, cultures and belief-systems in a comparative and child-friendly manner. This programme is designed to teach children about values, morality, social responsibility and rights, all of which are necessary to inform a child's developing mind to live in our rapidly changing society. Respect and appreciation for diversity is encouraged and being different is taken for granted.

In tandem with this ethos, the boards of management cannot promote or favour any particular religious persuasion. If parents wish their children to receive particular religious instruction or sacrament preparation, the school will fully facilitate this outside of the main class hours. In such instances parents get together and organise to have their children taught by a suitably qualified instructor after school. The school acknowledges and encourages interest in the various special occasions and festival days which may be celebrated by children of different religions. However, there is no one particular religious doctrine taught during school hours and in this way no child is forced to leave the classroom, to be "an outsider", while a religious lesson which conflicts with his or her family's own beliefs is taught.

Although Educate Together schools may seem to be a new idea, multi-denominational education has, officially at least, been present in the Irish educational system since its inception. When Lord Stanley introduced the national school system in 1831, it was originally envisioned that all schools would be multi-denominational, with religious instruction taking place separately. Unfortunately, the state took a very *laissez-faire* attitude to setting up schools itself, preferring to support church-led, local educational initiatives. In this respect, all the Churches must be commended for their efforts in getting the Irish national school system off the ground during the nineteenth century. However, this approach meant that the entire educational system rapidly became denominational, with each organised religion given the freedom to establish and manage primary schools under its own patronage and attended by members of its own faith. To date the state has not directly established any new schools itself — it is still left up to local groups to ascertain the need for a new school and to get one up and running before any state assistance is granted.

In recent years, however, more and more parents are becoming aware that they do have a right to choose what type of education their children receive and are increasingly turning to Educate Together to fulfil this right. The Irish state has repeatedly subscribed to the right of parental choice regarding children's education, in both national and international legislation. Article 42.3.1 of Bunreacht na hÉireann states that "The State shall not oblige parents in violation of their conscience and lawful preference to send their children to schools established by the State or to any particular type of school designated by the State." A subsequent government led by Eamon de Valera as Taoiseach signed the First Protocol to the European Convention on Human Rights in 1953 which states that "In the exercise of any functions which it assumes in relation to education and to teaching, the state shall respect the right of parents to ensure such education and teaching in conformity with their own religious and philosophical convictions." The Irish delegate at the time even went one step further by going on record to say that in the view of the Irish government Article 2 of the Protocol was not sufficiently explicit in ensuring to parents the right to provide education for their children in their homes or in schools of the parents' own choice. This Protocol has finally been incorporated into domestic legislation with the entry into force of the European Convention on Human Rights Act (2003). With such strong guarantees, at first glance it would seem that parents opting for multi-denominational education should have no problem finding such a school nearby. Unfortunately, in the greater number of instances, this is not the case.

Enrolment and Resources

To ensure that Educate Together schools are equally accessible to children from any social, cultural or religious background, each school operates an enrolment policy that is predominantly "first-come, first-served" and is not limited by religious preference or catchment area. All children therefore are equally welcome and their rights are respected from the outset. Individual schools may choose to reserve places for adopted children, siblings of pupils or refugee children, depending on the school's particular circumstances. However, the guiding principle is that every child has an equal right of access to an Educate Together school. Many Educate Together schools are over-subscribed and currently have extensive waiting lists for places. Therefore it is advised that parents put their child's name on the relevant school's pre-enrolment list as early as possible, in some cases within three months of birth. Each school has a designated pre-enrolment officer to whom any enquiries regarding places should be made. The lack of places in Educate Together schools, as well as in other national schools throughout the country causes considerable anxiety for parents in the run up to the start of term. Educate Together is working continuously with the other education partners and with the Department of Education and Science for better planning in school provision as a matter of urgency.

In common with other education partners, Educate Together deplores the under-funding of primary education in Ireland. All over the country, Educate Together schools can be found housed in old scout dens, rugby clubs, a golf club bar, converted barracks, community centres, a business campus and too many prefabs to mention. On the other hand, some of our schools that have secured permanent buildings through years of negotiation and fund-raising have gone on to win architectural awards. The Department of Education and Science has created measures to tackle issues such as substandard school buildings and to target disadvantage but the national picture with regard to the establishment of new schools is far from satisfactory. As described earlier, the State does not set up any new schools itself preferring to react to local initiative. On paper there is no distinction between proposed religious schools or multi-denominational schools. However, both groups are denied funding until the proposed school is up and running. This apparently "equal" treatment mitigates severely against groups who wish to set up multi-denominational schools. Treating all groups equally does not make for an equal outcome particularly in the Irish education system and the result to date has been far from fair. It does not reflect the growing demand for the differing needs of the youngest members of our population.

Educate Together as a national organisation fully supports, with representation and advice services, local Start-Up groups who wish to establish multi-denominational schools. The voluntary groups of parents are faced with the daunting task of setting up a school, with very little resources at hand, from scratch. Such groups of parents have to find suitable accommodation and pay various professional fees from architects, surveyors, etc. They also must organise a pre-enrolment list with at least 20 pupils to ensure viability and be eligible for grants. Once approval has been granted, the Start-Up group becomes the acting board of management and can proceed to recruiting a principal and first teacher for the new school. Opening a new multi-denominational school is by no means an easy achievement and requires considerable commitment from the parents involved; many Start-Up groups experience delays and disappointments before their vision is ever realised.

In spite of these difficulties, every year new groups of parents decide that a multi-denominational education is the best option for their children and they proceed to take up the challenge of opening a new school in their local area. The reasons quoted for choosing an Educate Together school as opposed to sticking with the traditional denominational models, which are much more widely available, all tend towards two aspects. On the immediate level, the ethos of Educate Together clearly demonstrates to parents that these schools firmly have the best interests of the child at heart. In a multi-denominational, inclusive educational environment, Educate Together schools seek to enhance each child's self esteem and creativity. Many of these schools choose not to have a uniform and encourage teachers and children to interact on a first-name basis, thus allowing the democratic principle to flourish within the classroom. All Educate Together schools are co-educational and actively strive to counter gender stereotypes from the earliest age, to the benefit of both boys and girls. This child-centred approach is often what first attracts parents to Educate Together schools. Taking a more long-term view, parents are also more acutely aware that Ireland has now become a rapidly diversifying society and will be a very challenging environment for any child to grow up in. These parents simply feel that if children are not segregated on religious grounds and instead learn together in a multi-denominational setting from the earliest age, being taught to appreciate and respect diversity, they will be better prepared to fulfil their individual potential as teenagers and adults in a multi-cultural society.

Educate Together is promoting and developing a national network of multi-denominational schools as a response to the changes taking place in our society; however, we would strongly argue that this is something that should have been included in the Department of Education and Science's strategy from the outset. Instead, it has been left to voluntary groups of parents to initiate and build this network. Without a doubt the movement has been successful and Educate Together has developed from three founding schools to become the fastest-growing sector of the education system today. Already there are groups working on plans for second-level Educate Together models. However, much greater state support is needed if the demand for places in existing schools and for new schools in new areas is to be fully met.

Educate Together is dedicated to promoting a future in which the concepts of equality, cherishing diversity and human rights become the fundamental foundation of the practice of education in Ireland. Through co-operation with the state and other partners in education, Educate Together hope to ensure that the concepts of child-centredness, inclusion and equality of esteem are transferred into the comprehensive reform of the entire education system. Educate Together will continue to promote high-quality, inclusive education and to work with their partners in education, to develop a modern integrated and inclusive education system in Ireland. The success of the Educate Together sector to date indicates that changing the education system is possible, for the fulfilment of all children and families in Ireland.

For more information, including some useful downloadable publications, visit the Educate Together website at www.educatetogether.ie, or contact Deirdre Mangaoang, Team Assistant, Educate Together, H8a Centrepoint, Oak Drive, Dublin 12; Tel: 01-4292500; Fax: 01-4292502; info@educatetogether.ie.

Private or Independent Schools[5]

This sector comprises those schools which are not state-funded. They range from fee-paying schools run by religious orders to small family-run schools that have been set up to cater for junior classes. Some are standalone primary schools while others are attached to secondary schools. They range in size from 30 pupils to over 330 pupils. They also vary in age, from schools that have been in existence over 100 years to newcomers that have opened in the last few years. Some school buildings are purpose-built for primary education, some are adaptations. Non-aided schools usually charge fees to fund themselves. Fees can range between €2,000 and €4,000 per year. There are two primary boarding schools.

The difficulty with explaining the ethos of the independent sector is that it encompasses a wide variety of establishments and while there are some similarities they all have their own characteristics. It is therefore wise just to make some broad generalities. Every school has established patterns of behaviour, routine and interaction, which contribute to what may be described as a school rhythm. Such schools are in the main very happy family-type schools with many second- and third-generation families attending, where parents choose to send their children, often travelling a great distance and making personal sacrifice so that their children can attend an independent school. Often parents relocate so that their children can attend the same school that they did.

In independent schools, the educational environment offered varies widely: big or small, denominational, non-denominational or multidenominational, co-ed or single sex, day school or boarding. However, they have many things in common, the aim always being to provide pupils with a caring stimulating environment within which they receive a wide range of balanced learning opportunities that meets their needs and lays the foundation of their future lives.

---

[5] This overview was submitted by Michael Troy of the Association of Independent Junior Schools, which has a membership of 31 schools and does not represent all private schools.

Independent schools follow the 1999 Curriculum as set out by the Department of Education and Science. In addition, it has always been part of the educational philosophy of educational schools to supplement the core curriculum on offer, recognising the need for breadth, balance, relevance, differentiation, progression and continuity.

As in other sectors, schools are organised in classes from junior infants to sixth class. There is no selection or streaming by ability; the schools are mixed-ability schools catering for all pupils. In the larger independent schools there are several classes at each stage. In the smaller schools pupils of a number of different stages may be combined in one classroom with one teacher. Average class size is 20 pupils but depending on the school and indeed depending on the class the size can range from 10 pupils to 30 pupils. However it would be the norm that class sizes of infants from first and second class would be small. Class sizes can increase as the pupils progress.

Differentiation of work is achieved by using various teaching methods including individual, paired, group, whole-class and thematic approaches. Pupils are involved in listening, reasoning, problem-solving and recording. Teaching methods take into account the range of ability, knowledge and skills in the class and the experience they bring to their learning. A variety of assessment tools, ranging from the informal to the formal are used to monitor pupil attainment and progress.

The bigger independent schools share facilities with senior/ secondary schools. This gives them the benefit of excellent extra-curricular and sporting facilities. The expectations of parents may be quite high in this area in particular with schools that benefit from a shared campus with a secondary school. It is generally accepted that independent schools are expected to provide a "value-added" element. Parents are paying twice over for their child's education and therefore can be forgiven for hoping that their child will receive that extra something from an independent school. It is part of the independent schools' philosophy that the variety of subjects and activities available to the children should be as diverse as possible to enable all children to find an outlet for their talent and potential.

What do parents want and what do independent schools offer to today's educational landscape? Here are just some of the issues:

- *Small classes definitely count.* Parents continue to want their children taught in reasonably small groups. This is particularly important in primary schools.

- *Ethos and culture count.* Most parents are making a choice for a child of four years where the focus is not on league tables (not as yet anyway). Rather, they have a wider vision of school and educational experience where there is a whole child integration of activities. Independent schools may find it easier to achieve this, because they are that bit freer, that bit more oriented to what real people want rather than what government departments order. After-school care, extra-curricular activities, and a longer school day may meet needs of parents both of whom work.

- *Teachers count.* Quality of learning reflects the quality of teaching. Independence allows these schools variety and diversity in the employment and deployment of staff. Different types of schools have different teaching needs, from Froebel and Montessori to subject-based and specialist teachers for subjects like PE, Music, Drama, Languages, etc. The staff are sufficiently qualified and experienced for the roles they are required to undertake in these schools. Often extra-curricular dedication is expected as a matter of course.

- *Communication counts.* Individual focused responsiveness — not just at yearly parent/teacher meetings — is one of the luxuries you get with a good private school. It is, many parents say, worth paying for. Some schools operate an open-door policy and others meet parental needs by having parent/teacher meetings on Saturdays. Regular reports and feedback are provided to parents weekly, at end of term and end of year.

- *Discipline counts. Pastoral care counts. Continuity counts.* The sharing of a campus and facilities ensures a smooth transition for pupils to second-level education in the school of their choice. All pupils transfer to second-level education.

The Association of Independent Junior Schools can currently be contacted c/o Michael Troy, Terenure College, Dublin 6W.

Special Schools

Throughout the State there are 125 special schools, which as the name implies provides education for pupils with special needs. The ownership and structure of these schools, which cater for about 7,000 pupils, vary: some are owned by Health Boards and may be attached to hospitals; some by the Department of Education; others by religious organisations or voluntary bodies set up to provide for a particular area of special need. Special needs education is such a large area that it needs a chapter all to itself — see Chapter 7.

Chapter 6

THE 1999 PRIMARY SCHOOL CURRICULUM AND YOUR CHILD AS A LEARNER

Paul Conway

INTRODUCTION

"What did you do in school today?"
"How did you do in school today?"
"How is my child doing compared to the rest of the class?"

When a child starts school in junior infants it is as much a land-mark event for the parents as it is for the child. From the very start of a child's school life, parents, more often than not, ask questions to find out about what school means to them. The three questions above capture some key aspects of curriculum: *What did you do today?"* asks about content and various activities of the school day. *"How did you do in school today?"* asks about how a child is doing; that is, how well their son or daughter is learning — an as-sessment question. Parents bring these questions to parent–teacher meetings, often adding a third question at that point: *"How is my child doing compared to the rest of the class?"* All three questions are about curriculum.

Your child's grandparents or maybe you yourself went to school when "reading, 'riting and 'rithmetic" — the 3Rs — was the curriculum. Nowadays, the curriculum is broader and more likely to be about the 3Ls — "living, loving and learning". The idea that a broad, balanced and holistic curriculum is important for a child's personal and social development has been a strong and valuable feature of Irish primary education for at least the last 30 years.

This chapter provides an overview for parents of the *Primary School Curriculum* (PSC), which was launched by the then Minister for Education and Science, Micheál Martin, TD, in September 1999. The launch followed a major review of the curriculum for primary schools by various partners in education building on the issues raised by the Primary Curriculum Review Body (1990), the National Education Convention (1994), the *White Paper on Education: Charting our Education Future* (1995) and the Education Act (1998). The 1999 revised *Primary School Curriculum* builds on the 1971 *Curaclam na Bunscoile* (Primary School Curriculum). The Primary School Curriculum reflects the educational aims and values of Irish society for primary school students, and assists educational partners in planning educational experiences for students by identifying learning guidelines and objectives, as well as suggesting preferred teaching methods. The 1999 *Primary School Curriculum* recognises very clearly the crucial role parents have in both supporting their children as learners (in and out of school) and in helping in the implementation of the curriculum itself in schools.

The 1999 *Primary School Curriculum* is available in a number of formats: in hardcopy as 21 books from public libraries and the Government Publications Office; and as downloadable files from the National Council for Curriculum and Assessment website (www.ncca.ie). The Introduction to the *Primary School Curriculum* provides a very good overview of how your child's learning is related to the curriculum and is well worth reading for parents who want to understand what the PSC is trying to achieve. Chapter 5 of the Introduction gives a general idea of what is involved in each subject area in the curriculum. A 44-page guidelines booklet, entitled *Your Child's Learning: Guidelines for Parents*, prepared jointly by the Department of Education and Science (DES) and the National Council for Curriculum and Assessment (NCCA) is available from the Government Publications Office. It outlines the seven curriculum areas, encompassing 12 subjects areas, in the Primary School Curriculum (see Box 1 below), as well as providing suggestions for parents as to how they might help their child learn in school.

Box 1: The 1999 Primary School Curriculum

Language
Gaeilge English

Mathematics

Social, Environmental and Scientific Education
History   Geography   Science

Arts Education
Visual Arts   Music   Drama

Physical Education

Social, Personal and Health Education (SPHE)

Religious Education
(As noted in *Your Child's Learning: Guidelines for Parents*,
the development of the curriculum for religious education
remains the responsibility of different religious bodies)

Compared to the 1971 Primary Curriculum, the 1999 Primary School Curriculum foresees a greater role for parents in contributing to their children's learning both at home and in school. In addition, the PSC encourages parents and the school to work collaboratively in supporting children's learning.

The 1999 Primary School Curriculum is both an extension of but also different from the 1971 Curriculum in important ways. It is extends in the 1971 curriculum in that it emphasises the *importance of the individual child,* and also puts a lot of emphasis on the child's immediate *environment as source of learning*. It is different from the 1971 curriculum in that some subjects are given a new or more prominent status. Science, for example, as well as Social, Personal and Health Education, are both more central to the 1999 curriculum. In the 1971 curriculum, some of what is now identified as science would have been included in what was then called Social and Environmental Studies. And some of what is included in SPHE could have been undertaken as part of health education in Physical Education. The greater emphasis on both of these areas reflects changing awareness about what is important for children to learn as Irish society changes. For example, the development of the science curriculum at primary level is seen as providing a ready supply of students who will enter post-primary schools ready to study science and ultimately enter science-related professions, and support the development of a more research- and knowledge-driven Irish economy. To take another example, as society changes at an ever-increasing pace, Social, Personal and Health Education (SPHE) has become more important in schools as society increasingly recognises that schools have an important role to play in supporting children's personal development, and that children need to learn new ways of relating to each other and of looking after their health.

This chapter is organised into three main sections as follows:

- What is curriculum and what is its role in a changing society?

- How can you support your child as a learner?

- Supporting your child as a learner in each subject area.

The next section starts with a story that helps highlight some important aspects of curriculum in a changing world.

What is Curriculum and what is its Role in a Changing Society?

Long, long ago, in a time before the Ice Age, there lived a teacher named New Fist, who taught activities such as "scaring a sabre-toothed tiger with fire", "horse-clubbing" and "fish-grabbing" as practical and relevant knowledge appropriate for getting ahead in those times. Elders and parents were happy with this curriculum for generations. However, years passed, the Ice Age came, and these skills no longer had direct relevance for the well-being of the tribe, which began to suffer. Radical thinkers, in the spirit of New Fist, proposed new subjects, such as "hunting big animals with spears". Many of the elders and parents did not agree, saying that the "old curriculum", that is, "tiger-scaring", "fish-grabbing" and "horse-clubbing" were taught for the general qualities of courage that they instilled in students. Indeed, they argued that these qualities of courage are relevant for all generations, despite changing conditions. Furthermore, some made the case that the best way to teach "animal-spearing" was to ask elders to tell stories about successful hunting while others argued that students needed practical experience spearing animals. Others made a strong case that society needed to know how successful students were in learning to spear big animals.

This story has some important insights in understanding the introduction of a new curriculum. First, curriculum reflects people's shared sense of the challenges they meet as a community at a particular time (e.g. fish-grabbing, living and working with computer technologies, how to understand the conflict and peace process in Northern Ireland). Second, the content of the curriculum is often seen as important for the society's very survival. In the above story, the coming of the Ice Age presented new environmental challenges for parents and children alike. Third, while people might agree that the curriculum is important for survival (to catch fish or to compete and contribute in a globalising world), they may disagree, especially as times change, about what skills to delete from the curriculum (e.g. fish-grabbing) and what new skills ought to be included (e.g. chasing animals with spears; learning to use computer technologies). Fourth, parents have both a point of view and an important stake in the curriculum. Parents have ideas about what ought to be taught, how it might be taught and the outcomes. Finally, the elders/parents had to talk to each other about what and how the curriculum ought to be taught, as well as how it might be assessed.

In Ireland, the National Council for Curriculum and Assessment (NCCA) is the statutory body whose job it is to advise the Minister for Education and Science about developments in curriculum and assessment. The National Council for Curriculum and Assessment was established in November 1987 as a successor to the Curriculum and Examinations Board and was reconstituted as a statutory body in July 2001. The brief of the statutory Council, as outlined in the Education Act (1998), is to advise the Minister for Education and Science on matters relating to ". . . the curriculum for early childhood education, primary and post-primary schools and the assessment procedures employed in schools and examinations on subjects which are part of the curriculum" (Section 41.1 a, b). The NCCA uses a broad definition of curriculum, which includes both specific content, outlined in the Primary School Curriculum, as well as other aspects of curriculum such as a school's ethos and cultural environment, which also teach important lessons to students. The NCCA states that "curriculum in schools is concerned, not only with the subjects taught, but also with how and why they are taught and with the outcomes of this activity for the learner". In relation to primary education, the Primary School Curriculum sets out specific *concepts, skills, areas of knowledge* and *attitudes* which children are expected to learn at school as part of their personal and social development. This chapter will outline these aspects of curriculum: what is taught and why, as well as the outcomes for the learner — a particular concern for parents among others.

While the Minister for Education formulates the curriculum, on the advice of the NCCA, others have important roles in curriculum at national and local levels. For example, at a national level, the Department of Education and Science (DES) Inspectorate oversees the implementation of curriculum. The DES Inspectors undertake whole school evaluations (WSEs) to learn about how schools are implementing the curriculum and provide suggestions as to how the individual schools might improve its work (see also Chapter 1). The focus of these WSEs is on the school rather than the work of individual teachers. At the local level, each school is required to develop and continuously update a school development plan. Section 21 of the Education Act 1998 requires each school to outline how it will address the needs of students with learning difficulties.

The 1999 PSC places a heavy emphasis on understanding your children as learners. The next section discusses some *key ideas about learning* and how you might support your child as a learner.

How Can You Support Your Child as a Learner?

Children learn both in and out of school. Learning in school presents different challenges for children than learning out of school. Out-of-school learning tends to be more active and practical; occur through social activities; use tools; and include social support often involving play. On the other hand, learning in school tends to focus on individual learning; involve mental work (often memorisation) with abstract symbols such as letters and numbers; and do so in situations where learners may often not have much support. For parents who want to support their children as learners, it is important to recognise that school presents real challenges for your child. All children will at some point find learning in school a somewhat different experience than the type of learning they might be familiar with at home or in the community. For example, a child being taught to fish at a local river or cook at home by another family member or friend will spend more time engaged in the actual activities of fishing and cooking than on reading books about each. In school, it is likely that learning about fishing and cooking will involve more individual and abstract work for learners. Some children will arrive at school more prepared than others for the different type of learning that occurs in school. Parents may have to adopt somewhat different strategies in supporting their child's learning both in and out of school.

One of the potential challenges of the current emphasis in society on performance and achievement, in which academic success in school can be crucial, is how to strike a healthy balance between ensuring that children experience childhood as a time of play as well as one focused on school work. Many child psychologists, for instance, argue that play, even if it appears informal and undirected (e.g. children's street games, language games, pretend play, formal games, etc.), has a crucial role in helping children prepare for adult roles and responsibilities, fostering children's social development, as well as supporting the development of thinking and problem solving. Thus, as parents endeavour to provide a good preparation for their child both before the child starts school, as well as during the school years, it is vital that time for play is valued and protected.

In seeking to promote a child-centred approach to teaching at primary level, the 1971 *Curaclam na Bunscoile* adopted five principles:

- The full and harmonious development of the child

- The importance of making due allowance for individual difference

- The importance of activity and discovery methods

- The integrated sense of the curriculum

- The importance of environment-based learning.

Similarly, building on the insights of the 1971 curriculum, the 1999 Primary School Curriculum focuses in considerable detail on learning, emphasising the child as a learner. Promoting a love of learning among children as preparation for life-long learning is a centrepiece of the curriculum (see Box 2).

Box 2: Children learn best when . . .

The PSC notes that children learn best when:

- they are actively involved in learning, that is taking part in interesting and stimulating activities;

- active learning gives them a deeper understanding of what is learned and helps them to remember it;

- learning arouses curiosity and harnesses their sense of wonder;

- they experience success in learning and gain a feeling of achievement, which raises their confidence and self-esteem and fosters in them an enthusiasm for further learning.

There have been many important developments in the learning sciences since the 1971 curriculum such as a greater recognition of the importance active learning, more emphasis on learners assessing their own learning, development of learning to learn strategies, emphasis on assessment as an integral part of teaching and learning, and a greater emphasis on language as a tool for thinking. These and other insights on learning are included in the 1999 PSC. The PSC identifies guiding principles about learning underpinning all subject areas. That children have opportunities at school for *active learning* is the most important idea about learning in the 1999 Primary School Curriculum. Opportunities for active learning are meant to encourage children so that *learning is enjoyable and engaging*. So, for example, across subject areas the PSC talks about how teachers will provide opportunities for children to think and work like scientists, historians, geographers, and writers in order to develop "habits of mind" that will be useful both in school and beyond. The PSC emphasises a number of important ideas in promoting active learning, which are outlined below.

The Individual Child

Noting that no two children are alike, the curriculum encourages the individuality of each child, including children with special needs. Although not noted in the curriculum, the research over the last 20 years on multiple intelligences reminds us that people have more than linguistic and mathematical intelligence, the two types of intelligences traditionally emphasised in schools. From the point of view of multiple intelligences, children have six other intelligences: musical, bodily kinesthetic, interpersonal, intrapersonal, spatial and naturalist.

Skills

The curriculum identifies different skills that are developed in every subject. It also notes that other key skills such as observing, communicating, asking questions and exploring are taught across subjects. Thus, in helping your children to develop these skills, teachers will be encouraging them to be good observers, to ask questions, to make good guesses, to investigate, to gather evidence and to make an argument. All of these processes are meant to develop "habits of mind" in children that will support them as learners in post-primary education and beyond in a changing world.

Developing Concepts

Concepts are big ideas or notions that help us understand the world. For example, in Maths children might learn that multiplication is a form of repeated addition (e.g. 3×5 is the same as 5+5+5). Or in Science, children might learn that the rotation and tilting of the earth on its axis, rather than the distance the earth is from the sun, explains why we have seasons.

Different Ways of Learning

The PSC recognises that children learn in different ways. Children learn from interacting with others in pairs and small groups, being taught in whole-class format by the teacher, and taking on different roles as a learner.

Working Together to Learn

One of the biggest insights from learning sciences over the last 30 years has been the role of "others" in supporting children's learning. Others here include the child's peers, parents, teachers and other people with whom they interact to learn knowledge, skills and concepts.

The Importance of Language

The PSC recognises that children learn languages such as English, Irish or other languages which they may have learned at home, but also that children learn *through* language. The curriculum notes that language plays a key role in the development of concepts. So, for example, in learning about the meaning of "mother" a child may learn that "ma ma" is his or her mother. Later, the child will learn that some, but not all, other women are also mothers. With more time and numerous opportunities to hear and talk about concepts and examples, the child may learn about the meaning of "motherhood", "motherland", "mother nature" . . . etc. The key point here is that language and concept development go hand in hand.

Literacy and Numeracy

Reading, writing and arithmetic — the 3Rs — was the way people talked about the central role literacy and numeracy play in school and society. Nowadays, literacy and numeracy are seen as more than basic skills but complex and high level skills themselves. The PSC emphasises both their importance and how language plays a crucial role in the development of both literacy and numeracy.

The Environment

Like the 1971 curriculum, the PSC notes that a child's immediate world of home, family, locality and community will have an important influence on how the child understands him/herself and the wider world. So, for example, children living near a canal may have particular set of experiences visiting, observing and being curious about canals. Teachers will try and build on these out-of-school experiences to support your child's learning of key curriculum concepts.

Hands-on Experience

Children's opportunities to learn are enhanced when they have a chance to handle, play with and try out ideas on objects and materials. So, in school, teachers will, throughout the primary years, provide materials with which children can explore and develop knowledge and skills.

An Integrated Curriculum

As adults, we are familiar with the idea of knowledge packaged into different subject areas. As adults we often learn and understand more clearly when we can connect ideas in one area with another. Likewise, children will benefit from being able to make connections between subject areas.

Assessment

The PSC emphasises the importance of giving parents a clear indication of their child's progress in relation to the curriculum. The PSC also emphasises the role of assessment in teaching and learning. Providing feedback on progress children have made as learners is now more clearly recognised. Thus, as children learn to write they may be asked to redraft or rewrite some piece of work based on feedback from the teacher. This in-class feedback is likely to help your child develop an understanding of the standard of work expected as well as help them set goals as a learner.

Information and Communication Technologies (ICTs)

The PSC notes the crucial role which ICTs play in today's world and the role they can play in supporting your child's learning. Over the last decade, efforts to integrate new ICTs into classroom teaching have been a common feature of education systems all around the world. Ireland has been no different. ICTs can provide opportunities for children to access information, communicate with other children and adults, visualise difficult concepts and express themselves more easily in words and images. ICTs are seen as important in preparing students both to learn in new ways and in order that they might fully participate as workers and citizens in a world increasingly shaped by new and more powerful digital technologies. For example, I recently heard a school principal talk about how a new computer-based "draw and paint" programme was transforming the way he was teaching art (fewer water jars and less paint spillage!) but also changing what he was able to teach about colour, shape, line, pattern, space — all elements of the visual arts curriculum. The National Centre for Technology in Education (NCTE) (www.ncte.ie) provides guidance and support for schools in the use of ICTs.

SHARING REFLECTIONS ON LEARNING

An important goal of the PSC is the promotion of a love of learning in children. As a parent, you can model for your child what it means to both think about and love learning. More so possibly than in the past, people of all ages have to learn about new things in their daily lives: ways to live with new technologies; new ways to relate to people who are different from us, including immigrants; and ways to re-train as jobs and working tools change beyond recognition. In addition, adults will have many memories of learning — both positive and negative ones. Share some of these with your child — both memories of your learning as a child and also your thoughts on you *as an adult who continues to learn*. You may be surprised how useful it is for both you and your child simply to talk about how you approach a new task (e.g. hobbies, work projects, learning to use a new tool or piece of computer software), how you organise yourself, how you seek help from others, how you check on your work/hobby to see if it is what you want it to be, how you perhaps struggled initially with a task but stuck at it and now feel more competent, and how you think about new things you will have to learn in the future. The point of these reflections and conversations is to help your child become more aware of how they engage with learning, as well as to help them see how they might *learn ways to learn* from others in their environment at home and school.

A further benefit of sharing reflections about learning arises when you have the opportunity to *share your expertise as a learner* in a particular area. For example, you may like to read a lot or make a particular recipe. By expressing your thinking aloud for your child, you are engaging them in an apprenticeship in thinking; that is, helping them to think like an expert reader, writer, cook, gardener . . . etc. So, for example, good readers often re-read a difficult paragraph, guess what might come next, or try to figure out the meaning of something they are not sure of in the text. Children can benefit enormously from adults regularly taking the time to share such "expertise" as the child and adult engage in shared reading at home. For younger children, in the case of reading it may be as simple as pointing to, and thinking aloud, how you might learn about a book's contents — i.e. looking at a table of contents, chapter titles, reading back flap. These are simple but crucial "ways of thinking", often a mystery to children who are new or even not so new to books.

SUPPORTING YOUR CHILD AS A LEARNER
IN EACH SUBJECT AREA

Supporting your child as a learner in and out of school is a very important part of your role as a parent in implementing the curriculum. An important issue for many parents, since they see school textbooks every day, is how to understand and use textbooks to support their child's learning.

The Role of Textbooks

Books are a central part of any child's experience in school. Indeed, the heavy weight of schoolbooks is a daily reminder of this fact! Despite the easy availability of resources through computers, it is unlikely that the book will be replaced by the computer. Rather, books and computers can be used to complement each other. The internet can provide more up-to-date information than that published in books in many instances.

In general, across all subject areas modern schoolbooks are more colourful, include more pictures, diagrams and graphs than older textbooks. These changes in textbook presentation can play an important role in helping children understand important curriculum topics. As parents see how textbooks are used in the Primary School Curriculum, they may notice a new relationship between textbooks and learning (see *Your Child's Learning*, p. 42). The content of textbooks and how they are used has changed and will undoubtedly continue to do so. Teachers will use textbooks as resources and often use more than one textbook in a given subject. In the past, teachers and classes may have used one textbook only, for example, in history or geography. You can help your children get the most from textbooks by talking to them about their books. For example, talking to your child about the pictures and diagrams in the book and how they help in understanding the written text can be of benefit to children of any age.

Over the eight years that your child will spend in primary school there will undoubtedly be times when learning particular topics proves challenging. For example, some parents may notice that on entering first, third and fifth class, their child is talking about some concepts that appear new. This may occur since the primary curriculum is organised into two-year blocks, so that a given set of issues are addressed in the four two-year blocks: junior and senior infants; first and second class; third and fourth class; and fifth and sixth class. It is also important to note that each two-year block builds on knowledge, skills and concepts addressed in the previous two-year block. As such, parents should not feel unduly worried if their child does not master new material as quickly as parents might expect, as children will have many opportunities to broaden and deepen their knowledge of key aspects of the curriculum over the course of a number of years.

Keeping in mind general ideas on learning outlined above, this section outlines the seven curriculum areas (12 subject areas), and identifies what parents can do to support their child as learner in each area and each subject.

Language: Irish/Gaeilge and English

The PSC recognises that language is the primary means through which people communicate. Language is especially important in school and life: language is essential to learn in itself as a way of communicating but also it is through language that students learn other subject areas. For parents, then, the way in which they use language at home, talk about Irish, French and other languages, can influence how their child's learning develops. The 1971 curriculum placed a strong emphasis on language and its role in children's education. Going further, the 1999 curriculum identifies language as a tool for thinking, a powerful mode for expression and as a way of making life more human.

Irish

Parents reading this chapter will be thinking of one of three different settings in which their child is learning English and Irish/
Gaeilge: schools in which English is the mother-tongue of their
child and the principal language of teaching in the school; schools
where Irish is the language of the home and the school (Gaeltacht
schools); and scoileanna lánGhaeilge, where Irish is the language
of teaching/instruction but may or may not be the language of the
home (see Chapter 5). Depending on the type of school that your
child is attending, the Irish/Gaeilge curriculum will be different. In
both scoileanna lán-Ghaeilge and Gaeltacht schools the curriculum
provides a setting in which Irish is the primary language of the
school experience and children are expected to reach a high level
of competence in Irish. In schools where English is the main language of instruction/teaching, students are expected to learn Irish
to a level that will support its development at post-primary level.

There are four parts to the Irish/Gaeilge curriculum: listening,
speaking, reading and writing. Consistent with principles of language teaching, the PSC approach to teaching Irish adopts the
communicative approach. In contrast to focusing on grammar and
translation, the communicative approach emphasises students'
contact time with the language and using it for "real-world" purposes. So, the curriculum puts a lot of emphasis on various tasks
and life-like settings in learning language. Children are likely to
be involved in games, conversations, role-playing, sketches and
drama as well as teachers focusing on how language can be used
informally in the classroom.

As a parent, you can support your child learning Irish/Gaeilge
at different stages. Before your child comes to school there is
much you can do as a parent to support what will happen when
your child starts to learn Irish in school, including:

• Using Irish words or phrases in everyday activities with your
  child.

• Using Irish — even if you only know some words and phrases
  — for communication with other adults and older children.

- Pointing to and noting when you see Irish words written or spoken on shopping items, on television (on the Irish language station TG4 or Irish language programmes on other stations), on the radio, on the internet.

When your child is in school, you can support their learning of Irish in a number of ways including:

- Talking about what your child is learning in Irish.

- Using some words and phrases being learned at school in the home.

- Asking your child to tell you words and phrases they are learning in school and using these at home.

- Using various word games, flashcards, and dictionaries available in Irish.

English

Many parents may think of reading and writing as the focus of English as a subject area. However, oral language — that is, speaking and listening — are important aspects of the 1999 curriculum. The ways in which speaking, listening, reading and writing are connected and can support each other is an important idea in the 1999 PSC. For example, as children learn to listen to rhymes, they develop skills in breaking down words into their various sounds. As children learn to write they learn how authors organise stories. As children learn to read they learn how they might organise an essay themselves.

As a parent you have a crucial role in fostering your child's language and literacy development from the first year of life. Before and after your child starts school you can:

- Pay attention to your child's efforts to communicate through words and gestures from their first efforts;

- Encourage your child to use a wide variety of words to talk about what is happening in their life at home, in their community and in their school. Talking about everyday experiences is important not only for language development but also for a child's personal and social development (see SPHE).

- Talk with your child both during and after television programmes; television provides many opportunities for language and literacy development.

- Read and tell stories to your child; pay attention to the stories your child likes and talk to them about why they like these stories.

When your child goes to school, formal teaching of literacy (both reading and writing) will begin gradually. Over the last number of years, the teaching of early literacy has focused on what is called *"emergent literacy"*. Emergent literacy recognises the way literacy develops gradually through opportunities to see literacy being used at home, the community and in school. Before children come to school, most will have become aware that the "strange squiggles" in books allow people to tell stories and pass on information. Some will be aware that books are read from left to right, that a book has a name, that some books have pictures, and that adults might tell a story while pointing their finger at the "strange squiggles" on the page. As a parent, you can support the development of reading in many ways:

- Read to your child; children of all ages like to be read a story from before they go to school to beyond the primary years.

- Show an interest in stories your child likes to hear and later likes to read.

- Read the newspaper yourself and encourage your child to read and talk about what is in the newspaper (e.g. you can start with the pictures/photos, and the TV page may also incite interest!).

- Encourage your child to join the local library.

- With increasing use of ICTs, books are now increasingly available online. If you have a computer, your child may be able to read some of the many suitable child-friendly online sites; supervision is of course essential. In Ireland, the National Centre for Technology in Education (NCTE) has been appointed as the Internet Safety Awareness Node for a European-wide Safer Internet Initiative. The centre will focus on raising awareness of internet safety issues among primary and post-primary students, their parents and teachers (www.ncte.ie).

- Depending on your child's interests and hobbies, provide books and/or magazines that will support both the development of the hobby/interest and reading.

As a parent you can encourage your child as a writer by:

- Writing notes to your child.

- Showing your child how you use writing in everyday activities e.g. shopping, writing down phone numbers, typing e-mail, reading letters from friends, reading bills!

- Encourage your child to develop an identity as a reader and writer by supporting them in writing to pen pals, writing text messages (they may need little support here!), and keeping a diary.

The importance of language does not end with English and Irish. Maths, for example, provides many opportunities to use language in relation to number, size, space, distance and other mathematical ideas that support the development of numeracy.

Mathematics

Recently in Ireland there have been concerns about high numbers of students who find Maths difficult at post-primary level. Maths is one of those subjects many people see as something they either have or do not have — "you are either good or not good at maths". It is important to emphasise that all children are aware of number, space, size, distance and other aspects of Maths in their daily lives before they come to school. Parents can do a lot in supporting their child's natural curiosity about each of these areas as they talk with them from before they start school. For example, every day there are opportunities to talk about size, distance, weight, space and number in the home, while shopping, while engaged in sports and while travelling. As a parent there are many ways you can support your child's development of numeracy:

- From the time your child is a toddler pay attention to and talk about number, distance, time, space, and shape. You can support your child's development of *emergent numeracy* by talking about and buying toys that will help your child to use language to describe shapes, distances and numbers, etc.

- Be patient with your child, as mathematical concepts can take children a number of years to grasp. For example, children may be able to count before they come to school but they more than likely will not understand number concepts until somewhat later.

- Use games as a way to introduce core mathematical ideas such as number, counting, sequence, etc.

- Teach your child songs, rhymes, stories and riddles as many include mathematical ideas and language e.g. "One two buckle my shoe, three four knock at the door"; the "Three Little Pigs" story can help children develop number concepts where there are repeated opportunities to think about and consider the number three.

- Use television programmes such as *Sesame Street* to teach both letters and numbers. Such programmes often provide numerous examples of how to introduce difficult concepts to young children.

Social, Environmental and Scientific Education (SESE)

Social, Environmental and Scientific is made up of three subjects: History, Geography and Science. History and Geography were prominent in the 1971 curriculum. Science is now given more emphasis in the curriculum. In addition, all three subjects begin in infant classes. History and Geography did not feature in the 1971 curriculum until around midway through the primary years. In all three subjects there is strong emphasis on the use of practical or hands-on activities in teaching. For example, the Science curriculum encourages practical investigation of everyday experiences children have with forms of energy, such as light and heat, living things, and the characteristics of different materials. There are a number of ways you can help your child in SESE:

- An important goal of the primary school years is that children gain a sense of place in the world. As a parent, you can support this goal by talking to your child about where he/she comes from, visiting places, and talking about what it means to live in a city/town, in Ireland (Geography and History), and in the wider world — Europe, the world (Science, Geography and History) and the universe (Science).

- Talking with your child about questions they ask that are of historical, geographic or scientific interest e.g. "How many years ago since the famine in Ireland?" (History); "Why are the streets so narrow in this part of the city" (Geography); "How come we see the lightning before we hear the thunder?" (Science).

- Be prepared to answer "I do not know" to some of the curious questions you may hear your child ask, but let them know there are different ways to find out e.g. look it up in a book or on the Internet; ask someone who might know; or go to the library and search in that section of the library.

- Encourage your child to engage with ideas related to history, geography and science through books, computer games, toys and television; and for older children, newspapers and magazines may also be useful.

- Pay attention to and talk about the rhythms of nature such as the seasons in terms of animal and plant life.

- Cultivate an interest in human endeavours that bring together science, geography and/or history. When I was a primary teacher, my class followed the journey undertaken by Dawson Stelfox and his team up Mount Everest in Spring 1993. Following that expedition with daily reports and a classroom wall chart provided many opportunities to talk about geography (Nepal's location; tallest mountains in Ireland, Europe, etc.; how mountains are formed) and science (human body's need for heat and oxygen).

- Care for the environment: get involved in, and involve your children in recycling and talk to them about how looking after our environment is important for all of us.

Arts Education

Arts education includes three subject areas: Visual Arts, Music and Drama.

Visual Arts

The aims of the visual arts curriculum are to develop children's observation (what they see, hear and feel) and critical (what they think/feel about art) skills, as well as their capacity to create or recreate what they see in their environment, mind or imagination. Visual art consists of six topics: drawing; paint and colour; print; clay; construction; and fabric and fibre. Consistent themes through all of children's exposure to visual arts in the primary years involve a focus on line, shape, form, colour and tone, space, rhythm and pattern. Children will be encouraged to talk about their own creations and you as a parent have an important role to play here. Asking children about what they have created, holding back from being judgemental but rather encouraging them to talk about why they created what they did are essential in fostering a language about the visual arts. There are number of ways parents can support their children in the visual arts:

- Think about and talk to your child about how the home, local area, shops, etc. are constructed by a combination of line, shape, colour and pattern. In other words, all the elements of the visual arts curriculum can be integrated casually into conversation with your child. This could also involve talking about clothes, beautiful sunsets, the moon, the shape and colour of birds or butterflies' wings, etc.

- Build up a collection of old magazines which your child can use to create collages.

- Many computers contain draw and paint programs, which can make an ideal tool for learning about shape and colour, as well as improving hand-eye coordination.

- Provide your child with materials, time and place to create and recreate art.

Music

Hardly an hour goes by in our daily lives when we are not exposed to music in some form or other, whether it is the jingles of a radio or TV advert, the latest pop chart hit, or the faint whisper of music from someone else's headphones on the bus or train. I once watched a totally engrossed three- or four-year-old child move in perfect rhythm to the songs of Andean street musicians, much to the amusement of the watching crowd. Children, typically, enjoy music in all its forms and make the link to movement very easily. Music in the primary curriculum is meant to develop the musical skills and appreciation of all students, and not just those who seem to have natural inclination towards the subject. The music curriculum consists of three areas: listening and responding; performing; and composing. In a similar fashion to the visual arts, music across the primary years will address certain basic elements: pulse, style, structure (same/different), pitch (high/low), and tempo (fast/slow). There are many activities a parent can undertake at home to support the music curriculum:

- Play music for your children on tapes or CDs, or play an instrument if you can.

- Sing and encourage your child to sing.

- Bring your child to musical events.

- Listen to your child and pick up on the music they seem to like and talk to them about this music. Ask them to tell you why they like it. You may need to help them with the language they use to describe their favourite music.

- Encourage your child to join a local music group or learn an instrument.

Drama

Drama is an important subject in that it supports the development of insight in different subject areas, and has a major role to play in supporting the development of the imagination. Children, like the little boy who danced naturally to Andean street musicians, are often naturally inclined to engage in make-believe play before they come to school at all. The best school can do is build on and extend, in important ways, children's natural capacity to engage in make-believe play. Parents can support children's "dramatics" by providing clothes and props to allow them to play out their various improvised scenarios.

Physical Education

The main aim of the PE curriculum is that children will learn to lead full, active and healthy lives. PE encourages children to have positive attitudes to sport and physical education. The curriculum recognises that each school will have to tailor its PE curriculum to its existing facilities whether they are modern or not so modern! In addition to focusing on the six areas of activity — that is, athletics, dance and gymnastics, outdoor and adventure activities, games, and aquatics — the PE curriculum also expects schools to develop children's understanding and appreciation of these six areas. PE, like the other subjects has knowledge and attitudes as well as skills as part of its focus. A key idea underpinning the PE curriculum is the promotion of *sport for all* children in the primary school, not just sport for the talented few. As a parent, you can support PE in the curriculum in a number of ways:

- Be a role model in terms of leading a full, active and healthy life.

- In an era where childhood obesity is a concern, encourage your child to take regular exercise. For adults and children alike, the same motto applies — "a little a lot is better than a lot a little".

- Encourage your child to *participate* in PE and other sporting activities.

- Acknowledge your child's achievements and progress in the area of PE, however small or large these may be. As the experience and recognition of competence is important to overall self-esteem, parents have an important role to play here. From a psychological perspective, children and particularly adolescents' self-esteem about their physique is a very important part of how they evaluate themselves as a person. In this case, then, it is especially important that you play an active role as a parent in supporting your child's physical self-esteem.

- Help out in various school sports and PE activities where such opportunities arise.

Social, Personal and Health Education (SPHE)

SPHE is one of the most important areas of the curriculum as it is concerned with the personal development of the child. SPHE is "caught" from the culture of the school as much as it is "taught" from the formal timetabling of an SPHE class. As such, the quality of the "school as a community" will influence what your child learns about SPHE. SPHE aims to teach children how to care for themselves and others. The links between home and school are especially important in SPHE for the teacher, the student, the parents and the school. SPHE consists of three themes: *Myself, Myself and Others*, and *Myself and the Wider World*. Consistent with the rest of the curriculum, teachers use *active learning* methods in SPHE. What kinds of activities might your child be involved in during SPHE? Discussion (especially), role-play, artistic activity, writing and use of multimedia to stimulate children's interest and engagement in the subject area are all important aspects of SPHE.

Relationships and Sexuality Education (RSE) is a central part of the SPHE curriculum. A report undertaken for the Department of Education and Science in the mid-1990s showed that there was a very high degree of consensus or agreement among parents that RSE should be taught in primary schools. As part of SPHE, schools can include the *Stay Safe* or *Walk Tall* programmes as part of their curriculum. The relationship between parents and the school is important in working out the approach to teaching RSE within the context of the school's ethos.

Parents have a number of important roles in supporting SPHE (including RSE) including:

- Keeping themselves informed about both the content and approaches to SPHE in their child's school.

- Recognising both your child's efforts and achievements and providing support for both effort and achievement.

- In a similar manner to the PE curriculum, emphasising the importance of a full, active and healthy life-style and the importance of misusing neither drugs nor alcohol.

- Communicating to children the importance of their family and the wider community and that children have a contribution to make in both family and community.

- Helping children to understand the changes that are happening in their body, in particular as they reach puberty and young adolescence.

- Encouraging and providing example of how children can develop good hygiene and good, balanced and healthy eating habits.

Religious Education

As discussed elsewhere, the Education Act 1998 provides a legislative framework for school patrons to define a unique ethos, promote such an ethos through appropriate policies and practices, and select key staff consistent with that ethos. As noted in *Your Child's Learning: Guidelines for Parents*, the development of the curriculum for religious education (RE) remains the responsibility of different religious bodies. It is up to you as a parent to decide the extent to which you want your child involved in RE. Any questions, concerns and suggestions in relation to RE should be addressed to the school.

A brief note on the history of how moral, literary and religious curricula have been understood in terms of curriculum is important in understanding current practices in primary schools. The existence of denomination-specific religious education curricula, directed toward the promotion of particular faith traditions in all but a few primary schools reflects the existence of a denominational structure in the management of Irish primary schools since the mid-nineteenth century. When Lord Stanley's letter established the national school system in 1831, the system was intended to foster good relations between children and families of different faith traditions (i.e. at that time between children from Catholic and Protestant families). Central to implementing this goal was the concept of providing combined moral and literary but separate religious instruction. By the mid-nineteenth century, within a few decades of Lord Stanley's letter, denominational groups had negotiated control of the national school system along denominational lines. As such, the denominational structure of Irish primary education has its roots in the mid-nineteenth century and these roots were recognised and strengthened in 1998 when the Education Act provided a legislative framework within which school patrons can foster a chosen ethos. Thus, in the Irish primary school context, the combined effects of historical arrangements and recent legislation have facilitated the maintenance and/or establishment of state-funded Catholic, Protestant, Muslim, Jewish, inter-denominational and multi-denominational primary schools. Schools managed by the Roman Catholic Church make up over 90 per cent of all primary schools in the Republic of Ireland, with the remainder of primary schools under Church of Ireland (mainly), Muslim (two schools),

Jewish (one school), inter-denominational (Foras Pátrúnachta), or multi-denominational (Educate Together) management.

In considering the teaching of religion in schools, it is important to distinguish between two different approaches: (a) the teaching of religion as part of preparation to *become a member of a faith community*; (b) teaching about religion(s) as a subject *like any other subject* (e.g. at post-primary level, religion can be studied as an examinable subject at Junior Cycle). In the first situation, where education for membership of a particular religious community is the focus, schools often draw attention to how religion permeates the wider curriculum. With the general decrease in religious observance across most, if not all, religious groups, schools are seen by many religious leaders and parents as important in fostering the unique tradition of a given religious faith.

Roman Catholic Religious Education

Primary schools under the management of the Roman Catholic Church use the *Alive-O* series of books. Like the curriculum for other subjects, the *Alive-O* series puts a strong emphasis on active learning. Children are often asked to reflect on their daily lives (e.g. talk about how important ideas are related to their own lives in school, home and community), create pictures/drawings or compose text that reflects insights gained from these reflections, or engage in role-play. The *Alive-O* series is designed to support integration with Social, Personal and Health Education and Relationships and Sexuality Education (RSE) curricula. The *Alive-O* series recognises that, for children, the most important signs of God are faith, prayer and the lives of Christian adults they live with and admire at home, school and in the wider community. The RE curriculum also seeks to foster faith by introducing children to simple Old and New testament biblical texts, liturgical feasts, the sacraments, and doctrine in the form of hymns, prayers, verses and simple statements.

Church of Ireland, Presbyterian and Methodist Religious Education

Schools under the patronage of the Church of Ireland, Presbyterian and Methodist Churches use the *Follow Me* series. The *Follow Me* series draws on the *Alive-O* series and has been adapted appropriately for different emphases in the Church of Ireland, Presbyterian and Methodist traditions. Like the curriculum for other subjects, the *Follow Me* series puts a strong emphasis on active learning. Children are often asked to reflect on their daily lives (e.g. talk about how important ideas are related to their own lives in school, home and community), create pictures/drawings or compose text that reflects insights gained from these reflections, or engage in role-play. The RE syllabus aims to enable children to develop a knowledge and understanding of beliefs, worship and witness of the Christian faith, and in particular of the Church of Ireland and other principal reformed traditions; to explore the biblical witness to God as Father, Son and Holy Spirit; to develop their own religious beliefs, values and practices through a process of personal search and discovery; and to develop an awareness of and a sensitivity towards those of other faiths and none. The *Follow Me* series is designed to support integration with Social, Personal and Health Education and Relationships (SPHE) and Sexuality Education (RSE) curricula. The *Follow Me* series includes much biblical material from the Old and New Testaments as well as songs, prayers and activities.

Muslim Religious Education

As of February 2005, there were two Muslim national schools in the Republic of Ireland, both of which are in Dublin. The first was opened in 1989 and the second opened in 2002. A religious education curriculum is taught in conjunction with the Arabic language and the study of the Koran. Students in senior classes participate in daily Duhr prayer, as well as observing Holy Day prayers each Friday.

Jewish Religious Education

There is currently one Jewish national school in the Republic of Ireland. The Zion National School opened in 1934 on South Circular Road, moved to Stratford College in 1980 and was renamed Stratford National School (Scoil Náisiúnta Stratford). A religious education curriculum is taught in conjunction with prayer, Hebrew, the Torah (five books of Moses) and general knowledge. The curriculum was developed by a Jewish religious education consultant involved in such work in England. The goals of the programme are as follows: to cultivate a love for Jewish learning, which leads to the development of virtues; to attain a proficiency in Jewish learning and practice; to nurture a pride in being part of the Jewish nation and appreciation of what this responsibility entails; and to provide rich and varied opportunities for pleasurable Jewish experiences, e.g. Shabbat celebrations on Friday morning.

Ethical Education Curriculum in Educate Together Schools

Learn Together, the ethical core curriculum for Educate Together schools, was launched in autumn 2004. The curriculum is divided into four strands: moral and spiritual development; equality and justice; belief systems and ethics; and the environment. Like the curriculum for other subjects, the *Learn Together* curriculum puts a strong emphasis on active learning. Children are often asked to reflect on their daily lives (e.g. talk about how important ideas are related to their own lives in school, home and community), create pictures/drawings or compose text that reflects insights gained from these reflections, or engage in role-play. The *Learn Together* series is designed to support integration with Social, Personal and Health Education and Relationships (SPHE) and Relationships and Sexuality Education (RSE) curricula.

WHAT ABOUT HOMEWORK?

In light of the emphasis in the PSC on parents' role in implementing the curriculum, it is important to address homework in this chapter, as the daily challenge of helping children with homework is often parents' biggest connection with the school curriculum and their child's learning. Homework can provide many benefits for children, parents and teachers. Children can develop a better understanding of material and become more independent as learners. Teachers can learn about how children and parents engage with the curriculum, and how well children have understood or learned the assigned material. Parents can learn about the curriculum, learn about how their child is getting on, and also see their child grow as a learner over the years. On a day-to-day basis, however, helping with homework can be demanding, as it competes with time for relaxation, play, or time with family members and friends — not to mention the television, mobile phone or computer! Many parents ask, "How can I help my child with homework?" There are a number of important points here:

- *Monitoring time.* Homework will typically involve practice or development of work undertaken that day in school. So, it should not take a huge amount of time. Children in infants and lower classes may get 10–20 minutes homework. As children progress through the primary school, they may get up to an hour by the time they reach sixth class. Of course, there may be times when older children spend a lot longer if they are engrossed in a project. As a teacher, I remember a parent coming in to tell me that her daughter and her friends had willingly spent two to three hours each evening during the week working on a group project on animals, even though it had not been assigned as homework. The children themselves told me that they weren't working for the full two to three hours but spent a lot of it talking to each other! Projects like that, however, are the exception rather than the rule in terms of time. Paying attention to what really interests your child is important in fostering their growth as learners.

- *Being aware of the work.* The nature of homework will differ considerably across the primary school years. Children in infants may be asked to finish a drawing, talk to one or both parents, or bring some object to school (e.g. photograph).

Children in upper primary years may have a variety of different homework assignments including writing, reading, a conversation with a parent or other family member, and some memorisation. Your child's teacher may talk about how you can help your child with homework.

- *Having patience.* It is important at this stage that homework be seen as an enjoyable and meaningful activity. So while taking it seriously, it is not meant to be a time when the child feels under pressure to perform. Learning can be rather up and down, and parents should not be unduly concerned if their child appears to have forgotten one week what they learned the previous week.

- *Keeping track.* As homework becomes more important over the course of primary school, most teachers ask students to record homework in a journal. Many also ask that this be signed each night by the parent after they have ensured that homework has been completed. As a parent, you have an important role to play here in providing a daily reminder to the child about homework.

- *Making connections.* As a parent you can play an important role in helping children see how homework can be meaningful. You may see connections between your child's homework and some family event or trip, or with your own work or hobbies. As the meaningfulness of curriculum is very important to foster, you can do this by helping your child make connections between homework and other everyday life as well as other school subjects.

- *Creating the right environment.* There are a number of practical arrangements you can make in creating a physical environment in which children learn from homework, including: providing a comfortable place to do homework (e.g. a place with little noise, sufficient heat, light and space all help); ensure that your child has sufficient rest; and check that the chair and table your child is using provide proper support and are not too cluttered. In addition, it is important to provide a space where your child can leave his or her bag and other school materials each day. There is little to be gained from a daily hunt for the missing schoolbag, homework or homework journal!

- *Avoiding conflict.* In addition to the physical environment, the social atmosphere is important. Homework should not be a daily battle of wills as to when and where it is completed.

- *Creating a routine.* Children will get the most out of homework if it is a regular part of the evening at home. Starting homework at the same time each day can be very valuable in teaching children the importance of routines and habits of work. Encouragement and praise are important in supporting your child's homework.

- *Keeping interested.* Show an interest in your child's homework and help your child see how it is valuable. Children may have to struggle a little as learners. It is important here to be attentive but not to get in the way of children's learning. Sometimes children can benefit a lot from working something out themselves with only some minor help from parents.

THE LEGAL BACKGROUND[1]

The authority of the state to prescribe the curriculum in recognised schools is found in Article 42 of the Constitution. Section 3.2 of Article 42 follows a provision that the state is forbidden to force parents to send their children to any particular type of school, and then states:

> "The state shall, however, as guardian of the common good, require in view of . . . actual conditions that the children receive a certain minimum education, moral, intellectual and social."

---

[1] This section was written by Oliver Mahon.

The 1998 Act addresses the curriculum in section 30, which provides that the Minister may "prescribe the curriculum for recognised schools" following a consultation process with school
patrons, national parents' associations, school management organisations and bodies representing teachers. Sections 39 to 41 of
the 1998 Education Act establish the National Council for Curriculum and Assessment on a statutory basis, indicate its composition
and appointments, and delineate its responsibilities. As noted earlier in the chapter, the NCCA advises the Minister in relation to
curriculum and assessment issues. The Minister is specifically
empowered, in section 30, to prescribe not only the subjects
taught, but the syllabus in each subject and the amount of instruction time to be spent on it, as well as matters related to guidance
and counselling that schools are to offer. A school is not, however,
limited to this curriculum. The section goes on to provide that, so
long as the prescribed curriculum is delivered, the board of management has the power to "provide courses of instruction in such
other subjects as the board considers appropriate". Furthermore,
Section 30 obliges the Minister to consider the characteristic spirit
of the school and not to crowd out of the school day subjects that
are related to that characteristic spirit by filling up all the available
instruction time with such prescribed material.

Nevertheless, it is clear from various provisions of the 1998 Act
that the delivery of the curriculum prescribed by the Minister, on
the advice of the NCCA, is absolutely central to the functioning of
a recognised school. One of the grounds on which the Minister
may withdraw recognition (see Chapter 1) is the non-performance
of the functions of the school, one of which is the delivery of the
prescribed curriculum. A less drastic step available to the Minister
in the same circumstances is to require the patron — and the patron must comply with such a requirement — to dissolve the
board of management, having first given the board notice of her
intention to do this and having then considered any representations made by the board as a result.

Clearly, the Minister is not short of muscle when it comes to
having the curriculum implemented in recognised schools. This

does not mean, however, that parents are merely silent and help-less onlookers in this process. The same section of the 1998 Act gives a parent a legal right of withdrawal of a student from "any subject which is contrary to the conscience of the parent". (This follows from a provision of the European Convention on Human Rights which states that the state must "respect the right of par-ents to ensure [that any education prescribed by the state shall be] in conformity with their own religious and philosophical convic-tions".) This is of course in addition to their constitutional right, referred to elsewhere, not to have a child attend religious instruc-tion. However, they do not have a right to have any subjects in-serted into the curriculum.

We can sum up the legal position therefore as follows: the Minister, on the advice of the NCCA, may prescribe matters relat-ing to the content of the curriculum and its delivery, and compel boards of management to ensure that these prescriptions are fol-lowed. The board has a limited power to insert certain subjects provided that the prescribed curriculum is delivered first. Parents have rights of withdrawal in certain circumstances.

CONCLUSION

This chapter provided an overview of the 1999 Primary School Curriculum and how you as a parent can support your child as a learner. The child as a learner is a key idea in the 1999 curriculum compared to the 1971 curriculum. As Irish society continues to change, curriculum will develop beyond what is outlined in the 1999 PSC. For example, given the fast pace of information and communication technology (ICT) change, the NCCA published ICT guidelines for teachers in 2003. These elaborate on how schools might integrate ICTs across the PSC. As a parent, you have a crucial role to play in supporting your child as a learner. First, each day you can provide support for your child as he or she learns about the world in and out of school. In paying atten-tion to what rouses your child's curiosity, what they find difficult, and when they make mistakes, you can promote a love of learning in your child that will support them in the school context. Second, you can play a role in local, regional or national parent councils/ meetings as well as provide input and feedback to schools in relation to curriculum planning in the context of School Development Planning (see Chapter 9). It is important to remember that the PSC outlines the official curriculum, and that each school and teacher will put the curriculum into practice in slightly different ways. As noted at the outset of this chapter, the 1999 PSC puts a strong emphasis on the role of parents in supporting their child as a learner and in implementing the curriculum. Both roles can be exciting and rewarding as both you and your child learn.

Resources

- DES/NCCA (1999), *Your Child's Learning: Guidelines for Parents*, prepared jointly by the Department of Education and Science (DES) and the National Council for Curriculum and Assessment (NCCA), and available from the Government Publications Office (01-6476834) or on the website of the NCCA: www.ncca.ie

- www.educationireland.ie/htm/education/main.htm — Provides an up-to-date overview of the Irish education system including primary education. This site was developed by the International Education Board Ireland (IEBI), established by the Irish government in 1993, whose remit is to facilitate and support the development of Ireland as an international education centre.

- www.scoilnet.ie — Network of Irish schools.

- www.into.ie — Irish National Teachers Organisation.

- www.edunet.ie — Provides links to education sites in Ireland.

Acknowledgements: I would like to thank Dr Fiachra Long and Lorraine Crossan for comments on a draft of this chapter.

Chapter 7

FINDING A SCHOOL FOR CHILDREN WITH SPECIAL EDUCATION NEEDS

David Carey

PREVALENCE AND CONDITIONS OF SPECIAL EDUCATION NEEDS

Estimates concerning the number of children who will have a special education need vary from country to country and depend on how these needs are defined and identified, as well as government policy. Reliable estimates are not available for the Republic of Ireland but a good rule of thumb is that somewhere between seven and ten per cent of children will have one form of special education need or other. If your child has a special education need, the search for a school is one of the most important decisions you will make as parents. The right fit between child, teacher and school is the best single predictor of educational success for all children and it is critically important for children with special education needs. This chapter outlines the conditions that result in a child being defined as having a special education need. After presenting this overview, the different types of school-based resources, and the different types of special education settings, are described. The significant factors affecting success in schooling for children with special needs are then presented. The author suggests questions and issues parents may need to raise as they make the difficult decisions about schooling. Finally, a brief outline of the current policy and legislative framework surrounding special education provision in Ireland is presented.[1]

Conditions that imply a special educational range from mild to severe, from low-incidence to high-incidence, and cut across all socio-economic strata. In Ireland the following conditions of special education need are officially recognised by the Department of Education and Science and carry with them an automatic entitlement to all the educational resources necessary to educate the child. In the context of this chapter it is not possible to describe in detail the signs and symptoms of each of these conditions but a brief, over-simplified description, taken from official Department of Education and Science guidelines, is provided below.

- *Borderline Mild General Learning Disability*: These children have been assessed by a psychologist and found to have an IQ that is in the range of 70–79. When they are experiencing persistent failure in the classroom they may avail of the services of a resource teacher.

- *Mild General Learning Disability*: These children have been assessed by a psychologist and found to have an IQ in the range of 50–69 and make slow progress in school.

- *Moderate General Learning Disability*: These children have been assessed by a psychological and found to have an IQ in the range of 35–49 and have significant learning difficulties and also social and adaptive difficulties.

- *Severe/Profound General Learning Disability*: These children have an IQ below 35 and usually have significant speech and language problems and associated physical disabilities.

- *Specific Learning Disability/Dyslexia*: These children have been assessed by a psychologist and found to have a level of intelligence within the IQ range of 90–110 (average) or higher. They

---

[1] Policies change rapidly and the information presented in this chapter is up to date at time of writing.

also have basic reading, maths or writing skills at or below the 2nd percentile (meaning 98 of 100 children will have higher skills) as measured by an individually administered test.

- *Emotional Disturbance and/or Behavioural Problems (includes ADHD)*: This category covers children who are being treated by a psychiatrist or psychologist for conditions such as hyperactivity, ADHD, conduct disorder, or other problems that disturb behaviour. It does not include children whose behavioural difficulties are adequately dealt with by ordinary school procedures on discipline.

- *Autism/Autistic Spectrum Disorders*: These children have been assessed by a multi-disciplinary team and found to have conditions that severely disrupt social interaction and behaviour such as autism or Asperger's Disorder.

- *Physical Disability*: This category refers to children who have conditions such as cerebral palsy, spina bifida, muscular dystrophy or who suffer accidental injury which limits locomotor or motor function often requiring special intervention and support to avail of education.

- *Giftedness/Exceptional Ability*: These children have been assessed by a psychologist and found to have an IQ well above the average range, usually above 130. Other definitions of exceptional ability exist and this is only the most basic criterion but one frequently used in the identification process.

- *Hearing Impairment*: Children with a hearing impairment are defined as having a hearing loss so significant that it impairs their capacity to hear and understand human speech, prevents them from participating fully in classroom interaction, and interferes with their learning. This category is not intended to include children with mild hearing loss.

- *Visual Impairment*: These children are defined as having a visual disability that is so serious it impairs significantly with the capacity to see; therefore they will have significant difficulty in mainstream classes. This category is not intended to include children whose vision is corrected satisfactorily by wearing eyeglasses.

- *Specific Speech and Language Disorder*: In the case of specific speech and language disorder it is a pupil's non-verbal ability that must be within the average range, with verbal skills well below average. Both a psychologist and a speech and language clinician must assess the child.

- *Children with Special Educational Needs Arising from an Assessed Syndrome*: These children have a diagnosed condition such as Tourette's syndrome or Down's syndrome. Generally it is required that a recognised specialist assesses the child and submits a report that documents the diagnosis. These specialists are often psychologists but can include speech and language therapists, psychiatrists, and medical specialists.

School-Based Resources for Children with Special Education Needs

Children with the above conditions may require a range of services from mild assistance to intensive ongoing intervention. The Department of Education and Science (DES) stipulates that the services provided to a child are consistent with the needs of the child and the degree of the condition's severity. Additionally it may be the responsibility of the Department of Health to provide some services such as speech and language therapy, physical therapy and occupational therapy.

The most important resource in supporting children with special education needs in school is the *human* resource, that is, the teachers. Although materials, equipment, and technology are often necessary, even critical, they are useless without qualified educators to implement them properly. There are four groups of people working in Irish primary schools who have as their remit supporting children with special needs. Three of these are professional educators: Learning Support Teachers, Special Education Resource Teachers, and Language Support Teachers; the fourth group are the Special Needs Assistants.

Learning Support Teachers

The Learning Support Teacher was formerly known as a "Remedial Teacher". Several years ago their name was officially changed to acknowledge their role as supports to children with learning difficulties. The Learning Support Teacher has a role to play with children whose academic achievement in Reading or Mathematics falls below a particular cut-off point when measured by formalised testing in school. Typically, children whose scores are well below average may be sent to the Learning Support Teacher for diagnostic assessment and if necessary direct teaching in the area of need. The assessment process is used to define a profile of the child's strengths and weaknesses in academic skills (there are times when social-emotional skills may be a focus of assessment as well).

Following the assessment process, the Learning Support Teacher is in a position to know if direct teaching, either individually or in a group setting, is necessary. If this is the case the Learning Support Teacher will organise a time to teach the child, in consultation with the child's classroom teacher. Learning Support Teachers specialise in educating children with learning difficulties or with some of the milder forms of special education need such as dyslexia or other forms of Specific Learning Disabilities. The time given to a child is based on the child's profile of need and usually extends over one or two school terms. The sessions, if the child is being taught outside of the classroom, average about 30 minutes each but often depend on the degree of severity of the academic difficulty.

Special Education Resource Teachers

These teachers are the newest addition to the specialists who assist children with special education needs in mainstream schools. Unlike Learning Support Teachers, the Resource Teacher may *only* work with children who have been assessed and found to have a special need condition. Their work with children is similar in many respects to that of the Learning Support Teacher; however, they typically spend more time in direct teaching, that is, provide more hours of intervention, than the Learning Support Teacher. They are responsible for assessment, direct teaching, and consultation with the classroom teacher, just like their Learning Support colleagues.

The Visiting Teacher Service

Specialist teachers who rotate through many schools may provide support for children with visual or hearing impairments enrolled in mainstream schools services. These teachers consult with the classroom teacher and work with the children individually if necessary. There is a visiting teacher service for children with hearing impairment and children with visual impairment.

Language Support Teachers

This newly appointed group of teachers assists children in Irish primary schools who do not have English as their first language. Some of these children may also have special education needs and will therefore receive support from these and perhaps other specialist teachers.

Special Needs Assistants

Some children with special education needs may require the services of a Special Needs Assistants (SNA). SNAs are not qualified teachers but many have undergone specialist training to undertake their positions. Their primary role is in supporting a child with physical or mobility difficulties, assisting in providing support on focused academic tasks under the direction of the class teacher, and accompanying children about the school grounds to assure appropriate peer interaction. Special Needs Assistants work under the direct supervision of the classroom teacher and are not meant to provide direct teaching responsibilities.

All of these resource staff in mainstream schools are under the departmental mandate to work in co-operation with parents, to review the effectiveness of their work, and to collaborate with the classroom teacher (the SNA works under the *direct* supervision of the class teacher). The type of support and assistance to be provided is dictated by the learning profile of the individual child and his or her unique strengths and weaknesses.

Types of Special Education Settings

In special education in Ireland, as in most other countries, there is a range of placement options available. The guiding principle for placement is what is known as "the least restrictive environment (LRE). The principle of the LRE mean that where a child with a special education need is educated depends on the individual profile of the child. Many children can be educated in mainstream classrooms; some will require more restrictive settings up to residential placement.

Under the principle of LRE a child will receive special education services appropriate to the degree of need. The principle extends from (in order of restrictiveness): the mainstream classroom with no additional support; mainstream classroom with specialist teacher assisting the child in the classroom; mainstream classroom and supportive services in another room from time to time; special class placement; special unit placement; special education school; residential school/facility; placement out of the country.

There are currently about 120 special education schools in Ireland. They are centres of excellent practice and should be considered a valuable resource to classroom teachers and parents. Children with severe special education needs may well require placement in a special school but this is a decision that should be made in co-operation and consultation with parents. The type of special school depends on the special education condition of the child and typically these schools cater to the needs of children with mild, moderate, severe/profound general learning disabilities, serious emotional and behavioural disorders, physical disabilities, schools associated with hospital settings, and schools for children with autistic spectrum disorders. There are also four schools for children with dyslexia (known as reading schools), three in Dublin and one in Cork. In these schools for children with dyslexia the pupils are educated for about two years and then returned to the mainstream classroom.

FACTORS AFFECTING SUCCESS IN SCHOOL

The severity of the condition has a major impact on successful schooling. There are children with special needs of such a magnitude that the goal of age-appropriate achievement in reading and mathematics may never be reached. It is important for all to recognise that, whatever the degree of impairment, success can be defined according to criteria beyond academic achievement, such as social interaction, ability to communicate basic needs, and ability to maintain basic adaptive skills such as dressing, feeding or toileting and meaningful, dignified interactions in the community.

The greatest single factor that will predict success in schooling for children with special needs is the attitude of the teacher responsible for the child's education. Although many professionals may share responsibility for the child's educational programme, it is an absolute requirement that the class teacher assume primary responsibility. What is important about this responsibility is that the teacher has reasonably high expectations for the child's improvement, is open to learning about the condition, is able to communicate frequently and openly with parents and other professionals, and takes on the responsibility to learn as much as they can about educating a child with that condition. Nothing is more important and nothing replaces the attitude of the class teacher.

The ability of the teacher to modify and change assignments, instructional strategies, class resources, methods of assessment and teaching style also influence a student's success in school. Children with special education needs often do not learn like other children learn. The teacher needs to be flexible in how she teaches and how she assesses the effectiveness of her teaching. It is important to remember that teaching children with special needs means that at times we must teach them to indicate when they are hungry, distressed, or need to go to the toilet. Special education is tailored to the needs of the child and there is no such thing as a one-size-fits-all programme. Everything must be tailored to the child's unique profile of strengths and weaknesses.

After the teacher the next most important person in the educational life of a child with special needs is the school principal. It is the responsibility of the principal to assure that everything possible is being done for the child and that every necessary resource has been acquired to implement the educational programme. The principal must have a strong commitment to including children with special needs in the school, have a flexible attitude towards discipline, be able to communicate clearly with parents, and be willing to join in genuine partnership with parents and guardians in the education of children with special needs.

Physical resources are also important. Some children with special needs will require specialised equipment and adaptations to the physical environment in order to succeed in school. Others will require assistance from professionals outside the school but who will work with the child in school and consult with teachers as needed. It is not always possible for a particular school to access all the necessary resources. When this is the case, difficult decisions must be reached, such as a change from mainstream classroom to special classroom or a change from mainstream school to a special school. These decisions need to be made in consultation, co-operation, and collaboration with the parents or guardians of the child.

Co-operation between parents/guardians and educators is an absolute necessity in the education of children with special needs. Parents may sometimes know more about the condition than the teachers and may know about educational interventions that are useful. On the other hand, teachers know more about how to create meaningful and appropriate lessons for children, including children with special needs, once they become familiar with the condition and its educational implications. By working together teachers and parents form a powerful partnership that increases the likelihood of successful outcome in school. Information must be shared openly and frequently. A home–school communication book is an important method of sharing and entries can be made daily if necessary. Teachers need to recognise that parents are frequently working with their children at home and it is important that the educational interventions being implemented in school are consistent with the interventions being utilised in the home. There must be a consistency between the activities of all parties attempting to work with the child. Neither teacher nor parent should feel threatened by the other.

The physical layout of the school is also a factor impacting on successful education. Children with mobility difficulties need an adapted environment. Classrooms need to be wheelchair-friendly and compatible. Books and resources need to be located in such a way that all children can access them. The classroom needs to be uncluttered with all resources organised in such a way as to orient every child to where they can locate important items. Children with autism need visually rich classroom environments where everything is identified in both words and pictures. They also need visual reminders of schedules and timetables.

Children with special education needs often have difficulties with peer relationships. The classroom and the school need to keep this in mind and be watchful for difficulties when and if they emerge. Successful peer interaction depends on the openness and attitude of children towards their peers who may be physically, cognitively or emotionally different. Teachers need to support children with special education needs in the social and emotional environment. A classroom environment in which mutual respect is given and received by all makes it more likely that all will get on well together. Children with emotional or behavioural difficulties need to be perceived as children with social problems, not as *bad* children. Social skills can be learned over time and teachers can teach social skills. Progress may be slow but progress can be made. Again, an attitude of reasonably high expectations and an outlook that anticipates ultimate success is important.

FINDING THE RIGHT PRE-SCHOOL OR PRIMARY SCHOOL

An inquiring and open mind and an ability to listen and read between the lines are the most important attributes a parent or guardian can have when trying to discover if a school is the right one for their child. Choices are limited by geographical and financial constraints and make it even more complicated. Despite this there are things a parent can and should do to ensure they are making the best possible choice.

If you are aware of another family that has a child with special needs enrolled in the school, talk with them. Find out how satisfied with their child's educational programme they are and ask about their experiences with principal, teacher, assistants and other school staff. Keep in mind that their impressions are highly subjective and may not be an unbiased account. However, if they are overwhelmingly positive or negative, it is communicating something of import to you. There is nothing to be lost and a lot to be gained from reaching out to the parent community and asking pointed questions about the school provided you are prepared to listen with a discerning ear.

Make an appointment to speak with the school principal. Don't hide the facts about your child's conditions but be sure you speak frankly about your child's strengths and don't focus solely on their difficulties. There is no need to hide the facts, just be sure you paint a complete and fair picture of your child. Answer questions put to you honestly and succinctly. Keep in mind what questions are asked. Don't introduce extraneous information, just answer the questions. The questions put to you will give you an insight into the principal's concerns about enrolling the child in the school. For example, if they focus on behaviour and discipline, then you will have a good idea that these may be primary concerns and may not match your child's educational needs. Listening between the lines is an important skill that all parents of children with special needs must acquire over time.

Don't be shy about asking the principal questions. You will want to know what experience he or she has in educating children with special needs. You need to know which teachers in the school have training in special education, either through advanced study, workshops, degree programmes, or real-life experience. There are specific special education training programme beyond the B.Ed. degree for primary school teachers. Ask if any of the teachers have these qualifications (Higher Diploma in Learning Support or Resource Teaching or Master's Degree in Special Education).

Enquire about the number of special needs assistants in the school and if any have a certificate or diploma credential. Ask if any of them might be able to assist your child if you think you need such assistance or ask about the process involved in seeking such assistance.

Share all relevant documentation concerning your child, particularly educationally relevant reports and assessments.

Ask if the school has children with special education needs currently enrolled and enquire about the nature of the conditions. It is important to get a feel about what experience the school has working with these children. You don't need to know the details, just try to get a general overview of the school's experience.

Ask if the receiving teacher has experience educating children with special needs. If possible, make an appointment with this teacher and begin the process of sharing and receiving information. Nothing predicts a successful outcome better than a successful beginning. Keep this in mind.

Ask if you can look around the school, particularly if you have a chance to visit the school while children are in attendance. You will get a "feel" for the educational environment that will inform your ultimate decision.

Be sure to enquire about what professional support is available to the teachers in the school. Is there an educational psychologist assigned to the school? If so, how often do they visit and what sort of support do they provide? Psychologists can be a wonderful source of help to children if their role is not confined to one of assessment only.

If your child requires one, is there a speech and language therapist assigned to the school? How often does he or she visit? How many children are on the caseload? A therapist with a caseload of 15 is certainly not going to be as effective as one with a caseload of five. These therapists are extremely helpful to teachers and children but supply and demand issues can limit their availability. Be prepared and understand that you will not always get the degree of help you need and it is not the fault of the school if this is the case.

Remember, the most significant and critical factor in successful schooling of children with special education needs is the attitude of the educators. You will get a feel for the attitudes of the professionals and assistants in the school quickly enough. Let it inform you about your ultimate decision.

THE IRISH CENTRE FOR TALENTED YOUTH[2]

The Irish Centre for Talented Youth (CTYI) works with young people of exceptional academic ability. Such students have been acknowledged by the Department of Education and Science as having "special educational needs". The Centre aims to address these needs by:

- Identifying high-ability students throughout Ireland through annual "Talent Searches";

- Providing services for these students, including Saturday classes, residential summer programmes, correspondence courses and Discovery Days;

- Giving support to parents and teachers;

- Carrying out research in this area.

The centre gives the following guidelines to teachers and parents to help identify those who might qualify under the term "exceptionally talented". It is important to remember that every child is an individual and so will have their own particular strengths, talents and weaknesses. However, exceptionally able children are likely to show some of the following characteristics:

---

[2] Submitted by the Irish Centre for Talented Youth.

- Keen powers of observation;

- Have learned to read early (often well before school age);

- Read rapidly and widely;

- Well-developed vocabulary — take a delight in using new and unusual words;

- Have great intellectual curiosity;

- Absorb information rapidly — often described as being like sponges;

- Very good memory — can recall information in different circumstances;

- Have the ability to concentrate deeply for prolonged periods;

- Very good powers of reasoning and problem-solving;

- Have intense interests;

- Possess unusual imagination;

- Have a great interest in "big questions", e.g. the nature of the universe, the problem of suffering in the world, environmental issues;

- Very sensitive — perhaps becoming upset easily;

- Very aware of rights and wrongs, concerned about injustices.

For more information, see contact details at the end of the chapter.

DEPARTMENT GUIDELINES, STRUCTURES AND LEGAL ISSUES[3]

Policies related to special education in Ireland change frequently. Parents need to keep current by accessing the relevant websites that are listed at the conclusion of this chapter. An overview of relevant documents can be helpful in providing parents with information helpful in negotiation their way through the special education maze of policies and procedures.

---

[3] These structures apply only to Irish primary and secondary schools.

In 1999, Minister Micheál Martin issues a department circular stating that all children with an assessed special education need have an "automatic entitlement" to all the necessary resources to enable them to succeed in mainstream schools. This circular set in motion a chain of events that continue to evolve to this day.

Since 1999, a large amount of human resources have been dedicated to special education. This includes the creation of new teaching positions such as special education resource teachers and language support teachers. Additionally a large number of special needs assistants were introduced into the system. Along with these new groups of teachers, a support service of psychologists, the National Educational Psychological Service was created. Although considerable difficulties have ensued in managing all these resources, they have had a positive impact on the educational provision for children with special needs.

A Staged Approach

Another significant department circular was distributed in 2003. This circular, number SP ED 23/04, outlined what is called a "staged approach to special education". It is an important circular indicating that there are three stages to allocating special education resources for children. At the first stage, if a teacher or parent suspects that a child has a learning difficulty in certain areas (academic, behavioural, emotional, physical or social), the class teacher must administer some observation or screening measures to assess the problem. Following this assessment, and working in co-operation with parents, the teacher must write a short, focused, intervention plan, and implement it over two full school terms, meeting regularly with parents.

If after two school terms there is no improvement, the teacher may, with parent permission, refer the child to the learning support teacher for diagnostic assessment. If the results of the assessment indicate the presence of learning needs, the child may receive services from the learning support teacher, again with parent permission. These services are to be provided over one school term.

If there is no improvement after one term the school may, with parent permission, refer the child for specialist assessment from a relevant professional such as an educational psychologist, speech or language therapist among others.

This staged approach to special needs provision is a major change designed to protect children from being assigned to specialists, small classes, or special schools when they may not require such interventions.

Structural Improvements

Within the last two years, structural improvements have come on stream. The National Council for Special Education (NCSE) was established in January 2005. One of the primary functions of the NCSE is to "consult with schools, health boards and other relevant bodies in relation to the provision of education and support services to children with disabilities". It must also monitor the progress of children with disabilities and ensure that they are reviewed at regular intervals and it is charged with the responsibility of making information in relation to provisions available to parents.

The Special Educational Needs Organiser (SENO) will be responsible for co-ordinating and facilitating delivery of educational services to children at local level. The NCSE, through the local SENO, will process applications for resource teacher support, special needs assistants, special equipment/assistive technology and transport.

Another function of the NCSE will be to identify the appropriate educational setting for children with special educational needs (i.e. whether the child's needs can be met in a mainstream school or whether they will need a special school). The NCSE will assume all responsibility for special education in Ireland in January 2009.

All of this information is taken from Circular Sp. Ed. 01/05 from the Department and parents of children with special needs would be well advised to obtain a copy either from their school or the Department (available online at www.education.ie).

The Special Education Support Service, based in Portlaoise, has been established to provide information, training and support to teachers and parents. This service is currently expanding its scope of operation and will be a major source of information in the future. These structures are new and it is reasonable to expect teething difficulties but despite this they all represent major changes and improvements in special needs provision.

Recent Legislation

There is also a legislative context for special education provision in Ireland. The Education Act 1998 provides a definition of special needs in legal terms in section 8 (and includes "exceptionally able students" in this definition), as described earlier. Section 20 of the Act requires schools to publish information related to special education provision. In general, the Education Act is an important document that specifies the legal rights of children with special needs to an appropriate education.

The Education (Welfare) Act 2000 provides protection for children that ensures they benefit from education, attend school, and in relation to all children, see to it that schools promote an environment that encourages children to attend and participate in the life of the school. Under the provision of this Act parents may, in certain circumstances, make complaints and seek the assistance of a Child Welfare Officer, if they believe a school is not performing its duty for a child with special needs.

The Equal Status Act 2000 protects the rights of the disabled from discrimination in educational settings. Among the disabilities defined are intellectual, sensory and physical impairments. The Act requires schools to provide "reasonable accommodations" to meet the needs of a person with a disability.

The Teaching Council Act 2001 regulates the teaching profession and seeks to improve the standards of teacher education and the professional conduct of teachers. Any person may refer a teacher to the investigation committee of the council if it is believed they have contravened the Education Act or the Education Welfare Act.

The Education for Persons with Special Education Needs Act 2004 is the single most important piece of legislation related to special needs. The Act specifies the procedures and processes that must be followed in providing services to children with special needs. The Act outlines exactly what is required in an "Education Plan" and provides for a process of parental appeal should they disagree with the educational provision of a child with special needs. It is important to note that at the time of writing this Act has not been implemented by the Minister into law (through the signing of a Statutory Instrument) and therefore has no legal status at present. This Act will become fully operative in January 2009, however.

In summation, there are a number of structures and acts that protect the rights and entitlements of children with special needs to an appropriate education. It needs to be noted that many of these are not yet fully implemented, some (the Education of Persons with Special Education Needs Act) are not implemented at all, and some contradict one another. Parents should always act thoughtfully in pursuing an appropriate education for their child. Speak with the class teacher first and be reasonable but assertive. Follow the recognised channels of communication from teacher to principal, to special education support team, to special needs organisers within the school before trying to bring matters to institutions outside the school.

SOURCES OF INFORMATION

There are a great many sources of helpful information as you go about trying to find the most appropriate school for your child. Use the internet to your advantage. A successful search will help you discover the specific questions you need to ask and the specific things you need to look for as they relate to your child's unique condition. Additionally, there are a large number of parent support groups in Ireland that are a tremendous source of information for parents and teachers. Do not be afraid to ring them up and ask questions. If they can't answer the question, ask them to refer you to someone who can. Among the helpful Irish support groups are the following:

- Caint (A Support Group for Speech and Language Imparied Children), 10 Bayview Drive, Killiney, Co. Dublin; 01-2823584.

- HADD (Hyperactive/Attention Deficit Disorder), Carmichael Centre, Nth Brunswick St., Dublin 7; 01-8748349.

- ASPIRE (Asperger Syndrome Association of Ireland), Carmichael Centre, Nth Brunswick St., Dublin 7; 01-8780027.

- The Dyspraxia Association, 54 Frankfurt Avenue, Rathgar, Dublin 6; 01-2957125.

- ACLD (Association for Children and Adults with Learning Disabilities, incorporating the Dyslexia Association of Ireland), 1 Suffolk St., Dublin 2; 01-6790276.

- National Children's Resource Centre, Barnardos, Christchurch Square, Dublin 2; 01-4530355.

- National Association for Parent Support, Capoley, Portlaoise, Co. Laois; 0502-20598.

- The School of Clinical Speech & Language Studies, Trinity College, Dublin 2; 01-6081496.

- Irish Deaf Society, Carmichael House, Nth Brunswick St., Dublin 7; 01-8725748.

- National Association for Deaf People, 35 North Frederick Street, Dublin 1; 01-8723800.

- Department of Education and Science, Special Education Section, The Principal Office, Athlone, Co. Westmeath; 0506-21363.

- National Parents Council (Primary), 12 Marlborough Court, Dublin; 01-6789980.

- The National Educational Psychological Service, Frederick Court, Dublin; 01-8892700.

- Irish Autism Alliance, 23 Summerfield Meadows, Blanchardstown; 087-9185002; www.irishautismalliance.com.

- Down's Syndrome Ireland, 30 Mary St. Dublin 1; 01-8730999 Locall 1890 374374.

- National Association for Cerebral Palsy (Ire) Ltd. Sandymount Clinic, Sandymount Avenue, Dublin 4; 01-2695355.

- National Association for Mentally Handicapped of Ireland, 5 Fitzwilliam Place, Dublin 2; 01-6766035.

- Irish Centre for Talented Youth, Dublin City University, Dublin 9; 01-7005634; E-mail ctyi@dcu.ie; Web: www.dcu.ie/ctyi.

- Irish Association of Gifted Children, IAGC, Carmichael House, 4 North Brunswick St., Dublin 7.

Important Websites

- *http://www.education.ie* — the website of the Department of Education and Science contains all the relevant circulars related to special education and the most recent special education legislation.

- *http://www.ncca.ie* — the National Council for Curriculum and Assessment contains new guidelines for educating children with General Learning Disabilities as well as the latest educational for the education of pre-school children.

- *http://www.into.ie* — the website of the Irish National Teachers Organisation is an important source of information for teachers and parents concerned with the education of children with special needs. It contains interesting commentaries on information included in the INTO and NCCA websites as well as information about teaching strategies for children with special needs.

- *http://www.sess.ie* — the website of the Special Education Support Service of the Department of Education and Science contains a host of helpful information regarding special education provision in Ireland and is an essential resource for parents and guardians of children with special needs.

Chapter 8

HOME EDUCATION

Kim Pierce

WHAT IS HOME EDUCATION?

This chapter will deal with home education, that is, children educated with their home as their base, rather than in a school (recognised or unrecognised).

Two words could be used to characterise home education: flexibility and choice. Parents[1] and children have the freedom to try out different ways of educating to find something that suits them both. They may alter these approaches over time to suit changing circumstances. Children have the potential to choose what they do, to a very large extent. This will obviously depend initially on their parents' view of education. Particularly when a child has been taken out of school, a school model tends to be carried on at home, as this is what both parent and child know. However, it is often the case that children, particularly younger ones, begin to resist the formality and methods of this type of education. When this happens, parents often start to change their approach and gradually move toward a more informal method,

---

[1] Please note, throughout the text the word parent will be used to include any guardian.

where the child has a greater degree of choice and control over what they do.

Not all home educators use informal methods, some may be fairly formal and structured as in school, but within this they may use project-based learning that does not artificially split their activities into separate, discrete blocks. In life, activities usually encompass a wide range of "subjects". For example, shopping includes maths, planning and social skills, among others. It could be expanded to include geography (where do products come from), biology (how is food produced) and politics (how does global trade work and what effects does this have on producers and consumers). This list is endless. Everything we do can be looked at in this way to see the areas of learning it includes.

Most families are happier using informal methods, where the child chooses what they do and the parent provides resources and stimulation. Some families combine both informal and formal methods. In all of these ways of educating, a central feature is conversational learning and individual attention. Perhaps the two most important criteria for home educators are that children enjoy learning and are happy. Such approaches help to make home education such a success. Children have their parent on hand to ask questions of, as and when they think of them. If the parent doesn't know the answer, a search can then begin that involves both parent and child in the learning process. Shared learning involving both child and parent is also common in home education. Much learning takes place through discussion. Parents may also provide opportunities for their children to join outside clubs when they show an interest.

Home education is a very interactive process and learning progresses at the child's pace. As an example, children may become fluent readers from anywhere between approximately two and 11 years old. In the home, late readers do not have any stigma attached to them and do not regard themselves as failures. Late reading can be due to a learning difficulty such as dyslexia but in many cases it just means that the child is not ready to acquire this kind of skill. When they do, they often become fluent in a very short space of time and go on to become avid readers. Some home educators have noticed that learning can occur in bursts, followed by periods of seemingly little activity. It appears that these periods of little activity are really times of assimilation and digestion. Children then seem to make large leaps in their understanding.

Dr Alan Thomas, a leading researcher into home education, is particularly interested in informal education and says in his book *Educating Children at Home* (1998, pp. 67–68):

> We do not even know much about informal learning in early childhood. It is taken for granted. It is only relatively recently that research into language acquisition has demonstrated how language is learned almost entirely informally. Apart from this, our knowledge of informal leaning is quite scant. The best support for the proposal that school-age children can go on learning as they did in infancy comes from parents who, when their children reach school age, just go on doing what they are already doing. They have certain unstated goals obviously, to continue to develop their children's oracy, literacy, numeracy, scientific, geographical and historical understanding, general knowledge, emotional maturity, social competence and physical skills. But these goals do not have to be spelt out any more than they did when their children were younger. These parents are simply continuing their children's apprenticeship to the culture. There is no reason why learning should have to undergo a radical change at the age of five or so. Neither does the curriculum of the culture suddenly have to be compartmentalised into relatively autonomous compartments as it needs to be in school.

Another important facet of home education is the ability to treat children individually. Families with several children may use different approaches for different children according to their needs. Children in the same family may acquire the same skill at different ages. Reading and writing are examples of these. One child learning to read at four whilst another reading at ten need not be a problem in a home educating family. The separation of children into "successes", "failures" or those with "difficulties" by continual comparison with other children through formal testing and assessment need not happen. At home parents do not need to formally test their children regularly to determine their progress. They closely interact with them on a daily basis and know exactly at what stage they are.

Likewise, the label of "late learner" need not be applied. Our culture places a strong emphasis on achievement, particularly academic achievement, at a young age with more value being placed on the child the younger they acquire any given skill. However, why should a child feel more valued if they learn to read at four, than at ten? In the long run, what difference does this make? The argument has been put forward that many parents would see late readers as being at a disadvantage and that they would need lots of catching up to do. My own belief is that the term "late reader" is an artificial one that unnecessarily labels children. The school system is viewed as normal and in it children are taught to read at a young age, as this is the main way that information is transmitted in schools. As a result, anyone who hasn't mastered the skills of basic reading by the age of say, five to seven, tends to be seen as being outside the range of "normal" and therefore as having a problem. In some cases, the child may have a special need such as dyslexia, but in others it may just be that the method of teaching reading doesn't suit them or that they are just not ready for this type of skill.

My eldest daughter was a late reader. I started to teach her to read when she was about six, as I was more locked into my own school conditioning of when children should be able to read. She didn't take to it easily and we struggled along for a while until her resistance was so strong that I called a halt. We did no reading for several months and I then tried again. During this time, we had read lots of stories as she has always enjoyed being read to. When we tried again, her reading ability had taken a large leap, despite doing no practice on it for several months. I came to the conclusion that the part of her brain that operates during reading just needed more time to mature. During the next few years, we dipped into reading at intervals. It was never very easy and she told me that she thought the English language was crazy, with all the exceptions to the rules, the letters that you don't hear, the letters that change the sound of other letters, etc. I remember reading that the English language has one of the highest rates of reading difficulty when compared with a language such as Italian, where there are no exceptions to the rules. My daughter is now 12 and is regularly found with her nose in a book.

If we view reading skills as just one of a range of information-gathering tools, amongst which are visual and hearing tools, then "late" reading need not be seen as such a problem. My daughter has an excellent visual and aural memory and has picked up lots of information about the world we live in through these means. Conversational learning tends to be a feature of home education and she has developed her vocabulary and critical thinking skills through extensive conversation as well as listening to and watching videos (we have a collection of nature and science films) and participating in practical activities such as gardening, cooking, etc. Her greatest difficulty with "late" reading was my attitude towards it. In her view it wasn't a problem; it only became one if I saw it as one. Looking back I realise that if we view the age of acquiring reading skills as being within a range of approximately two to 11 years old, then children do not need to be labelled or feel like they are failing. Unfortunately, it would be extremely difficult for a school to cater for this range due to its structure. At home, it need not become a problem.

WHY DO PEOPLE HOME EDUCATE THEIR CHILDREN?

Home educators fall into two categories: those who have never sent their children to school, and those who have withdrawn their children from school because of problems. Parents in the first group will usually have begun to investigate home education when their children were very young, sometimes before they were born. They may have begun to think about their own school years and wonder if there is an alternative. Some parents may have had an unhappy school experience themselves; conversely, some may have been very successful but have come to realise that that success only applied to a small percentage of students and at some cost to themselves. They want something different for their own children. Such parents will have read books and articles on home education and possibly talked to others who are already home educating. Some feel that school may limit their child because of large class sizes and a "one size fits all" approach. Others may wish to home educate for religious reasons. Some have children with special needs that they are successfully educating at home.

There are, of course, many parents who are very happy with the school that their child goes to and the child is making good progress, and home education may not be for them. However, parents who choose to remove their child from school do so for a variety of reasons. Home education is usually something they have never considered. If problems with school cannot be resolved, this is a choice they feel they must make for their child's well being. Some may feel that they can give their child the individual attention that is impossible for most teachers due to class size. There are many parents whose children may have a mild special need who do not do well in the school environment. Some children with autism, dyslexia or Down's syndrome, for example, benefit from a home environment that is flexible and are truly able to progress at their own pace without being labelled different, slow or difficult. Home educating such children is very challenging for the parent but reaps great rewards in happier children. Parents in this category often feel very stressed and question their ability to educate their children themselves. Despite this, such parents usually go on to become successful home educators once they have seen their children become happier and start to enjoy learning again.

Our culture places great emphasis on training and qualifications in order to fit someone for a particular job or career. This is crucial for some activities. However, as Dr Thomas says, "parents or carers do not need any special training or qualifications" (1998, p. 126). The whole area of education is still being researched and debated. The school model is only one of many models of education. Even among schools, methods of educating can be very different. Many home educators would like to see our culture develop to a point where home education is seen as but one of a range of options available to parents, and that these options are not seen to be in competition for greater value. The crucial task would be to choose an option that suited your child best. There should be the freedom to change options depending on circumstances.

THE BENEFITS AND COSTS OF HOME EDUCATION

The benefits of home education are significant. The home provides an environment where the child can learn at their own pace and in a style that suits them. Peer pressure is largely absent and bullying is not tolerated. Children have a parent on hand to discuss anything and everything with. They are not labelled and are not under pressure to achieve good results in regular tests. They are free to enjoy learning about the world around them and explore their own particular interests as far as they wish. Consequently they tend to be happier, more self-led, more confident and higher personal achievers. It is challenging and rewarding for parents, who get to spend a lot of time with their children and enjoy their progress on a day-by-day basis.

So, why doesn't everyone home educate? The costs are considerable. It takes commitment, time and real care to home educate a child. Parents must possess a willingness to assume the responsibility for helping a child every day through various experiences, some of which may be difficult or frustrating. Many parents do not feel capable of taking on this kind of responsibility, nor wish to. As mentioned earlier, our culture tends to place great emphasis on the expert or qualified person. Parents who don't have a third-level qualification or perhaps left school without the Leaving Certificate often feel that educating their own children beyond about five is too much for them. I think that they tend to forget that they helped their children to walk, talk, master the skills of dressing and eating by themselves, and in some cases have begun work on recognising and playing with numbers and letters. Some parents with an unsuccessful school background may feel they just don't have the ability to home educate. They themselves may have poor reading or written skills. I know of parents in this situation who are strongly motivated to home educate and find ways around these problems. They may go to adult literacy classes themselves; they may enlist the help of a friend or relative, buy or borrow a good set of dictionaries. Home educating their children may be the spark needed to improve their own skills.

On a more general note, having spoken to many parents, the initial decision to home educate is often the hardest part. Some parents find the decision so hard, because they see it as possibly isolating them and their children from friends and family. They may feel that they will be criticised or ostracised and that their children will lack playmates. In some cases, this has happened, as the belief that children can only be educated in schools is still overwhelmingly strong in many people. This makes a difficult start but children have gone on to make new friends and parents have found support through joining a network such as the Home Education Network and meeting people who sympathise with what they are doing.

In many cases, once the parents have made the decision and have been home educating for a few weeks or months, they find that they are capable and that the difficulties they might have anticipated just don't appear. Home educating in the early primary years need not involve expensive outlays on materials. Lots of learning happens through everyday activities. Even in the older primary years, expense can be kept down. A few well-chosen reference books can help the parent become more knowledgeable on areas in which they may be a bit "woolly". It has been said more than once that the educational background of the parent is much less important than their level of motivation. Being interested and determined, and finding creative ways to overcome problems, are more important.

The school system is free in the main and largely removes the responsibility from parents for the success or not of their child's education. Home education usually means surviving on one income as one parent needs to be with their children. This can be impossible for some families due to financial commitments. However, some single parents have also home educated, despite the obvious financial difficulties. Some people may feel that home education is only open to those with a "middle class" background and a good supply of money. People tend to forget that a huge amount of learning can be achieved with little or no cost. Children of any "class" may have problems at school that cause them to be withdrawn. If we look at education as something that arises out of general living, often using easily available everyday materials, the whole process becomes much less daunting. The best resource we have is our mind and developing its ability to think creatively. Lack of money can be a stimulus to finding creative ways to educate. Sometimes our attitudes and assumptions about who can educate, how education should happen and what "education" means can be our greatest obstacles.

Some would see education as the process by which skills and interests are drawn out of a person and then developed, where thinking skills are developed to enable that person to think creatively and flexibly and to excel at problem-solving. They would not necessarily see it as amassing huge amounts of information, which in large part may be irrelevant to their lives. There is too much information in the world for any one mind to hold. It has been said that is more useful to develop the thinking skills that enable a person to decide what information they may need and where to find it.

For those for which it is possible, home education does involve some expenditure on educational materials. However, many resources are free or cost little. Libraries are a source of free books, sometimes audio tapes, CDs, CD-ROMs, videos and DVDs. If parents have internet access, there are now many free educational resources, often aimed specifically at home educators. Walks in the woods (biology, botany) cost nothing; many science experiments can be conducted at home using ingredients found in the kitchen. If home educating families are geographically close enough, shared learning between families can happen where a parent with a particular skill may extend this to other families. Families may club together to pay a teacher for group work such as pottery.

Socialisation is one issue that often concerns new home educators, their families and friends. Some home educators have had a lot of pressure put on them to send or return children to school from well-meaning friends and family. These tend to feel that the children will be isolated and lack social contact with other children. However, most families have more than one child as well as relatives and friends with similar aged children. Why is it considered necessary for children to see other children of a similar age, every day, for several hours? There is no evidence to support the belief that home education means isolation and lack of socialisation. It is more an urban myth. Whilst being a fairly common attitude, it is a curious one because the opposite is almost certainly true in fact. There is some evidence to show that home education provides better than normal social skills, with more rounded abilities. Home educators make great efforts to provide their children with social contact. This may involve travelling to see other home educators, joining outside clubs, or getting involved with community projects. Many have friends who go to school that they will also meet up with. There is evidence from Dr Thomas's research in the Australian outback to show that isolation is not a problem. Dr Thomas found that in Tasmania some children live on homesteads huge distances from any other family. They would see any other brothers or sisters on a daily basis but would only often meet other children at two-week yearly camps. To his knowledge, no concerns were raised about their socialisation (1998, p. 112).

Play is a very effective way of learning, but it does not necessarily have to be between child and child. Children can play on their own or with adults. Adult–child play can be a very productive way of learning with the adult stimulating the child in ways that would not happen with same-age child play. Issues such as non-sharing, exclusion and bullying that can happen with child–child play, don't happen when adults are involved.

Dr Thomas has the following to say (1998, p. 124):

Home educated children obviously have less opportunity to mix socially with other children of the same age. But this does not appear to hamper their personal or social development, or the acquisition of social skills. On the contrary, most parents came to believe their children had a more normal social upbringing than if they had been in school. They pointed out that children in school experience very little adult social contact in comparison with home educated ones. More contentiously, they criticised the narrowing effects of being part of the same-age subculture in school, with its restricted view of the world and pressure, sometimes physical, to conform to its mores. It was also pointed out how the institution of schooling directly fosters the development of such a subculture. It is reasonable to ask whether school is the best place to learn social skills other than those obviously necessary for survival in school.

As Dr Thomas points out "very little research has been directed at social development" (1998, p. 112) but the anecdotal evidence of home educators so far indicates that home education produces socially competent children, able to converse with and relate to people of all ages. I know of home educated children who later attended secondary school or university with no problems. Some found the structure a little odd at first but adjusted. Some found that the structure treated them as much less mature than that found at home. The sociability of children depends to some extent on their innate character. Some children are outgoing, some tend to be shy. This applies to all children, whether they go to school or not. Home education can build confidence in children so that they are more able to deal with interpersonal issues such as bullying. I have heard it said that children need the "rough and tumble" of school in order to learn how to deal with life. I would disagree. I believe peer pressure and bullying just have a negative effect on children. Some bullied children become bullies in their turn; some children conceal their interests if they don't fit well with the dominant peer group interests. They don't tend to learn positive behaviour patterns that will help them lead a happy, productive adult life. My own daughter experienced mild bullying in one of the clubs she attends. She stood up to it and it didn't worry her or make her doubt herself. I think this is because she has a good deal of confidence in herself that we have taken care to build up and the bullying did not damage this positive picture of herself.

Some parents are confident about educating their children at home past the primary years but others feel less sure. In Ireland, it is possible for home-educated children to take Junior and Leaving Certificate through a distance learning school run by Nuala Jackson. Some may choose to take A levels through the UK-based National Extension College or the Dublin Tutorial Centre. If children initially decide to take a non-exam route there are still options available later to take courses and gain paper qualifications through evening classes and distance learning institutions such as the Open University. Students may also enter college and university as mature students.

LEGAL REQUIREMENTS[2]

Many people are unaware that the Irish Constitution gives parents the right to choose where their child is educated. The right of parents to discharge their duty to provide "for the religious and moral, intellectual, physical and social education of their children" is a constitutional right, explicitly stated in the first part of Article 42. The Article continues by stating that "parents shall be free to provide this education in their homes or in private schools or in schools recognised or established by the State". Any laws relating to school attendance must take these constitutional provisions into account.

For many years school attendance in this country was regulated by the School Attendance Act 1926, which compelled parents to cause their children of school-going age to attend a school on every day that the school was in operation. There were some stated exceptions to this general rule, such as illness of the chil-

---

[2] Most of this section was written by Oliver Mahon.

dren, lack of an available school or the receipt of education in some other fashion, and the means of enforcement was by way of fines in the District Court levied on the parents, with the final sanction, for persistent offenders, of taking the child into the care of the State. This Act saw education as a simple matter of enforced school attendance, and lasted, with minor amendments, until 2002, when it was repealed in its entirety by the current statute, the Education (Welfare) Act 2002.

The Welfare Act approaches school attendance and its enforcement from the point of view of conferring a benefit on the children rather than as a simple matter of the enforcement of the law. A new statutory body, the National Education Welfare Board (NEWB), has been established to deal with matters relating to the delivery of education. The NEWB has functions in relation to monitoring the educational provision of educators, in recognised schools, non-recognised schools or as individual home educators. It is early days yet but there are indications that the NEWB are considering taking a more supportive role in addition to monitoring, in their relationship with home educators. (One very welcome and potentially significant function of the Board is the promotion of an appreciation in society generally and in families in particular of the benefits of education and of the social and economic advantages that flow from it.)

Given that the Constitution provides that the parents have the option of home schooling, the Welfare Act has to balance the right of the state to ensure "that children receive a certain minimum education, moral, intellectual and social" (which is also provided for in Article 42) with the right of parents to provide education at home. The difficulty is that a "minimum education" has never been exactly defined, either in the Constitution, or by the Welfare Act. The Guidelines issued in 2003 by the NEWB, which provide a framework for implementation of the Welfare Act, seek to uphold parental right to choose home education whilst at the same time ensuring that children receive a "minimum education", as written into the Constitution. The Guidelines contain a "working definition" of "minimum education" which parents need to show the

NEWB they are delivering. This definition is broad and does not state exactly what or how to educate, or give age limits by which children might be expected to have achieved any given skills, such as reading or writing.

In order to balance these rights, the NEWB is required to draw up a register of all children who are being educated at home. In addition, the NEWB also keeps a register of all children attending recognised or unrecognised schools. (For the purposes of this Act, a child is defined as a person resident in the state who is over six years of age and who is either under 16 or who has completed three years of post-primary education. The effect of this is that the school-leaving age is now 16 or the completion of three years at a post-primary school. It had stood at 15 years for many years before this.)

The parent of a home educated child is obliged to have the child's name placed on the NEWB register, and must state where the education is being provided. Initially the parent should contact the NEWB to apply for registration. They will be sent an application form. Once this has been received by the NEWB, the parent will be contacted by the NEWB-appointed authorised person to arrange a preliminary assessment interview. This will be based on the information on their application form. It will take place where the parent chooses and their child need not be present. If, on the basis of this interview, the authorised person can determine that a "minimum education" is being provided, then the child will be included on the register. If there is some doubt, then a further level of assessment will be carried out. This is called a Comprehensive Assessment and will only be carried out where the NEWB is unable to determine, on the basis of a Preliminary Assessment, whether a minimum education is being provided.

The NEWB will then send "an authorised person" to carry out an assessment of the education being provided, the materials being used and the time being spent on providing it; this will be done in consultation with the parent. If the NEWB, having studied the report of its investigator, is still unable to decide this question, it can send its representative to enter the place where the child is being educated and observe the process of delivering the education, inspect any premises as well as any equipment or materials used to do this, and carry out an assessment of the child; all this is to be done with the consent of the parent.

The Act specifies that the assessment of the child will be of his or her "intellectual, emotional and physical development" as well as the "knowledge and understanding" of appropriate subjects and also "proficiency in such exercises and disciplines as the authorised person considers appropriate". Clearly therefore the assessment will not be a narrow one, focusing solely on proficiency in academic subjects, but will also seek to evaluate the development of the child as a person. A report of this assessment will be submitted to the NEWB, and a copy will then be sent to the parent who will be invited to make any representations he or she considers appropriate to the NEWB in respect of it. It is on foot of this report, and the representations (if any) made by the parent, that the NEWB will make a decision in respect of the adequacy or otherwise of the education being provided.

Having considered these matters, the NEWB has three options. The first is to register the child as a child who is receiving a satisfactory education outside a recognised school. The second is a conditional registration: the child will be registered subject to the parent undertaking to comply with whatever requirements may be laid down by the NEWB, which will be designed to ensure that the child receives an adequate minimum education. The third is a refusal to register the child at all. (If the child is attending an unrecognised school rather than being educated at home, and if the child's education is deemed to be satisfactory, all the children who attend at that school will be entered in the register without further individual examination provided that the school notifies the NEWB that they are receiving education at that school.)

If a child is successfully registered in this way, the NEWB is empowered to have the child assessed at intervals of the NEWB's choosing thereafter to ensure that the provision of education remains satisfactory, and can either de-register the child, or require that the parent gives undertakings in writing to ensure that the deficiencies in the education will be remedied.

If the child is registered subject to the parent undertaking to comply with the requirements of the NEWB, and the parent fails to carry out the undertakings given, the NEWB has no option but to remove the child's name from the register.

What if a parent refuses to consent to the child being assessed, or refuses to give such assistance as is required to enable the assessment to take place? The NEWB has a simple remedy: either to refuse to register the child or to remove from the register the name of a child who had been registered. Then the parent has no option but to send the child to a recognised school.

In the case of a child whose name is on the register, the parent has an obligation to inform the NEWB if any particular that is part of the register is no longer correct. In assessing whether the requisite education is being delivered, the NEWB may not de-register a child in cases where an illness of the child (temporary or permanent) is the cause of the non-delivery. Children who are receiving education outside the state are also outside the scope of the Act.

In cases where the NEWB has refused to register a child, has removed a child from the register or ordains that undertakings be given by a parent as a condition of registration, there is a provision to allow the parent to appeal any of these decisions to the Minister. The Minister is then required to appoint an appeal committee to hear this appeal, which must consist of a District Court judge, an inspector and another person to be appointed by the Minister. The appeal committee, having heard both sides of the argument, can affirm the NEWB's decision, compel the NEWB to register the child or compel the NEWB to register the child subject to the parent giving undertakings to comply with any requirement that the committee considers appropriate.

The registration of a child in the above way is an exemption for a parent from the general requirement in the Act to cause a child to attend a recognised school on each school day, and makes the parent immune from prosecution under the Welfare Act and from the substantial fines that can otherwise be levied on defaulting parents.

CASE STUDIES

Both of these case studies are UK-based but serve to illustrate experiences that can exist in any home educating community. They have been taken, with kind permission, from *Educating Your Child at Home* by Jane Lowe and Alan Thomas (2002, pp. 152–153 and 137–138). There are other cases where children took a non-exam route and went directly into employment that interested them.

Lois

> Very little education was planned as we were too busy living life and enjoying opportunities as they came along. When the girls were young they just played and played, and sometimes life seemed just like one glorious muddle. We believed in allowing natural development and we could see that they were bright, happy imaginative children who had a real enthusiasm for many things. We used to meet other home educators and we did all sorts of things together, and we were always busy. I wondered what would happen as they grew older but it seemed wrong to interfere and to try to control the unfolding of their lives.

> Time went by, and both of our daughters underwent a change in their thirteenth year. Our older daughter became interested in maths and she began to study it seriously. Other subjects followed and later we enrolled her on some distance learning courses for exams. She achieved impressive results at GCSE [Junior Cert level] and A-level [Leaving Cert level] and went to university to study maths. She is now completing a higher degree.

> Our younger daughter became interested in music at an early age and she was able to spend as much time as she wished on her playing. Practice was always a natural and unforced part of her life so we weren't really surprised when she decided that she wanted to take music seriously. GCSEs and A-levels were needed for her application to music college, so we had to get organised and study for them. It wasn't always easy and sometimes we used to

fight, but she succeeded. After gaining two A grades at A-level she threw herself into preparation for the audition four months later. She applied to two of the music colleges in London and was offered a place at both.

Naturally we are proud of their achievements but we've always placed greater importance on their development as sensitive and compassionate people. They have always made their own decisions and they have never been pushed. In fact, if an Inspector had descended upon us in those middle years it would have been very difficult to explain what we were doing in a way that would have made sense to someone who was steeped in conventional education. But the outcome has shown that we were right to trust our instincts.

Sam's Mother

Sam did go to school for the first two years but I soon realised that it wasn't working out. He was obviously bright and well motivated but I could see quite early on that he was struggling with writing, and his reading was not very fluent. Eventually I took him out of school because I could see that his enthusiasm was waning and I realised that matters could only get worse. We had to abandon everything associated with writing for some months, and I did a lot of reading to him instead of putting him under pressure to read for himself. I had to be very patient and it wasn't easy at all. He just couldn't make the connections between the sounds and the letters and he had great difficulty remembering the work we did on it.

I was reluctant to use the term "dyslexic" and he was very insistent that he didn't want to be labelled, but he does have great difficulty in this area. His reading did come on eventually and it was wonderful when he actually began to enjoy it and be excited by it. Writing remained a problem so we did lots of other things which didn't require it. When he was about 12 he began to show a talent for art, particularly pottery and all kinds of modelling. He really enjoyed his new-found creative interest and he also got his first computer at this stage. The computer became very important to him and his self-esteem improved quite a lot over the next couple of years.

Then he decided that he wanted to go to college to take his GCSEs and at this point he agreed that we would have to find some strategies to help him with the writing and spelling problem. We used some dyslexia materials regularly for about a year and this did seem to help. We decided that the best way was to focus on the artistic and practical subjects and others which required the least possible amount of writing, so he took Maths, Physics and Art first of all. In the second year he took English and IT and he was so pleased when he passed, especially the English. It was a real struggle for him but he was able to go on to a two-year course in Art and Design. I'm convinced that he would have given up entirely if he had stayed in school, but his problems weren't "bad" enough for him to have received any learning support.

Helpful Contacts

For more information, contact the Home Education Network, a non-denominational support and lobby group for home educators, c/o Kim Pierce, Carrowgar, Ogonnelloe, Scarriff, County Clare; Telephone: 061-923023, e-mail: kimpierce@eircom.net; Website: www.binf.org/hen/; or e-mail hen@www.binf.org.

Distance learning with Nuala Jackson: she provides Junior and Leaving Certificate courses and can be contacted on 051-383426 (evenings) or on her website at www.xlcproject.org.

Dublin Tutorial Centre: www.dtc.ie. Tel: 01-6612209.

National Extension College: www.nec.ac.uk.

Recommended Reading

Dr Alan Thomas (1998), *Educating Children at Home*, Continuum (available from the Home Education Network).

Jane Lowe and Dr Alan Thomas (2002), *Educating Your Child at Home*, Continuum (available from the Home Education Network).

Thomas Armstrong (1991), *Awakening Your Child's Natural Genius*, Tarcher/Putnam.

Grace Llewellyn (1991), *The Teenage Liberation Handbook*, Lowry House.

Dr Raymond and Dorothy Moore (1994), *The Successful Homeschool Family Handbook*, Nelson.

Jean Bendell (1987), *School's Out: Educating Your Child at Home*, Ashgrove Press.

Anything by John Holt, Maire Mullarney or Linda Dobson.

Chapter 9

Parents' Associations and Organisation

Communication with Parents

Parent–teacher meetings are an essential part of the partnership required to ensure the best outcome for a child's learning and development. Parent–teacher meetings are organised by the school once during the year. As part of the benchmarking process, the Department of Education came to an agreement with the teacher unions that meetings would take place half within the school day and half outside. In effect, this means that meetings can take place beyond the school finishing time but, unless different arrangements are put in place, meetings are still most likely within the working day of most parents.

The National Parents' Council (see below) has lobbied for meetings to be held in the evenings to accommodate more parents. If parents are worried about their child's welfare or progress, they are entitled to speak with the teacher at any stage and are normally encouraged to do so. It is understandable that school management would suggest that the parent makes an appointment with the teacher to allow them to set aside time for a satisfactory discussion and make provision for the supervision of the class.

Parents should be given copies of school policy documents which are relevant to them, such as the code of behaviour (including the policy relating to the disciplinary process) and admission policy (including admission of children with special needs). From time to time the department also issues circulars of interest to parents which should be circulated through schools.

Much communication from school of a routine nature is conveyed through notes given to the child to bring home. It is up to parents to check their child's bag regularly for notes, as schools cannot be held responsible for information not received. In the case of separated parents, it is vital at the beginning of the year to explain the circumstances to the class teacher so that no confusion should arise with regard to communication.

PARENTS' ASSOCIATIONS

In keeping faith with the Constitution (which states that the primary and natural educator of the child is the family), the Education Act 1998 brings parents very much centre stage as partners in education. Apart from the inclusion of two parents on every board of management, the Act specifies that parents may establish a parents' association.

The local association, once established, is bound by two strict rules: membership must be open to the parent of any student who attends the school; and the association must promote the interests of the students attending the school. The association is not entitled to act solely on its own initiative in promoting the students' interests; it must do so in co-operation with the management and staff of the school, as well as with the students themselves. It would follow that the ideal would be to have the association, the board of management, the principal, teachers and students all working in the interests of the students in a co-operative and harmonious spirit.

To enable it to achieve its primary purpose of promoting the interests of the students, the association is given two significant entitlements in relation to schools. The first is the right to advise the board of management or the principal on any matter that relates to the school; the second is to adopt a programme of activities designed to promote parents' involvement in the operation of the school. This must be done in consultation with the school principal.

To ensure that the advice offered is listened to, both the board and the principal are obliged to "have regard to" it; this, however, is by no means the same as saying that the advice has to be followed. What is required is that the board and/or the principal must consider the advice, evaluate it in the circumstances of the school, and if it (or some of it) can reasonably be taken on board, then that should be done.

A board of management is obliged to "promote contact" between the school, the parents and the community, and to "facilitate and give all reasonable assistance" to parents who want to set up an association, and afterwards to the association once it is set up. Clearly the statutory intention is that every recognised school should in time come to have an active parents' association, working to promote the students' interests in co-operation with management and staff. Section 6(g) of the 1998 Act lists parents specifically as people with whom schools must liaise and consult; and Section 6(m) commits the education providers to the enhancement of transparency in educational decision-making. Section 21(3) states that the school plan shall be prepared in accordance with such directions relating to consultation with the parents, the patron, staff and students of the school, as may be given from time to time by the Minister in relation to school plans. Clearly it makes sense for schools to seek the input of parents in areas such as code of behaviour, homework policy and Social Personal and Health Education.

The involvement of parents in the operation of the school can take many forms. Extra personnel are always needed at the time of school plays, concerts and the like. Sports days need stewards, as do school games, particularly in relation to transporting teams, and there are numerous other opportunities in the life of the school for parents to make a most valuable contribution. However, a note of warning should be sounded in relation to insurance. Volunteer parents would not, without a special arrangement being made, be automatically covered by a school's policy of insurance, and parents who volunteer, and schools which receive volunteers, should all note this fact, and make the appropriate arrangements, particularly in cases where parents provide transport for pupils in private cars. For this reason all parental involvement should be carefully planned in advance and structured in consultation with the insurers; this may not always be as straight-forward a matter as it might seem, but it is too important to pass over.

There are undoubtedly many ways in which such an association can confer a real benefit on the pupils, besides those mentioned above: homework clubs, coaching of games, organisation of all sorts of activities in many areas, clubs catering for various interests and hobbies and many others are all areas in which an organised group of parents can confer a real benefit on the pupils and enhance their quality of life.

Many parents' associations are the backbone of fundraising for extra resources or facilities that the board may not be in a position to provide from state funding. Associations are entitled to raise money to fund their own activities and develop their own organisation. Some associations organise lectures or courses of general interest to parents (e.g. parenting or Irish classes for adults). Formerly, most of what was done in schools was done by teachers; Section 26 of the Education Act 1998 enables parents to take a share in benefiting the pupils, by mobilising resources of personnel that the school on its own could never match. However, the requirement that any activities that involve parents in the operation of the school must be done in consultation with the principal, and in co-operation with the board, principal and teachers, must not be forgotten, bearing in mind that while the parents' association is entitled to advise, all management decisions can only be legally taken by the board. In addition, parents' associations have a valuable role to play in the development of school policies. Bearing this in mind, the co-operation between the association and the school should, if properly managed, never be less than fruitful.

THE NATIONAL PARENTS COUNCIL[1]

The National Parents Council Primary was set up in 1985, under the programme for government, as the nationwide representative organisation for parents of children attending primary school. NPC received statutory recognition in the Education Act 1998. NPC has charitable status and is a company limited by guarantee. It has a board of directors and employs a chief executive and staff.

NPC promotes and supports the work of parents' associations as set out in the Education Act. NPC is the representative organisation for parents. There are approximately half a million parents of primary school children, covering approximately 1,000 parents' associations in branches around the country. By getting involved parents can ensure that NPC is truly representative and that the voice of parents is strong and influential in the development of national policy and in the setting of funding priorities for state spending on education.

The Aims of NPC

- Improving the life chances of all children by promoting parental involvement and partnership in education at national, local and school level.

- Providing supports for parents to enable them to play a full part in their children's learning (including training programmes, materials and information).

- Empowering parents as primary educators through provision of information, awareness-raising, help and advice, advocacy, creation of local networks and opportunities for peer support.

- Enabling parents to have a say in their children's education, at national, local and school level.

---

[1] This section was submitted by Fionnuala Kilfeather of the National Parents' Council.

What NPC Does

- Advocating for parents;

- Bringing parents' views to bear on education policy (see below);

- Providing information services to parents;

- Providing a helpline and advocacy service for individual parents;

- Providing a wide range of training and support services for parents;

- Facilitating parents to develop peer support networks at county and local level.

How NPC Brings Parents' Views to Bear on National Policy

NPC is consulted on all important education issues and has representatives on primary education committees and boards established by the Department of Education and Science. NPC also represents parents on a wide range of child-, parent- and education-related issues and has made sure that the perspective of parents is brought to bear on national education policy.

NPC has been able to have an input into new laws that affect children and parents and has been successful in ensuring that much of the new legislation has a child's rights focus. NPC continues to advocate that all policy decisions must be made in the best interests of the child.

Through membership of the National Council for Curriculum and Assessment, NPC has been able to ensure that the curriculum now being delivered in primary schools reflects a modern parental view on what and how our children are taught and learn.

The development of the National Children's Strategy is welcome and the focus on democracy for children and the hearing of the voice of the child is very much in line with NPC policy. We believe that the democratisation of school for children and their parents is a key part of serving the needs of children and the country. NPC has worked hard over the years on issues such as a complaints procedure for parents and young people, a real voice for parents and children in whole school evaluation, the development of national strategy for children's health. NPC is greatly concerned by the number of children who have poor attendance at school or who drop out of school and has made an important contribution to the focus on child welfare in the Education Welfare Act and continues to work for a supportive welfare service for children and parents.

NPC is also concerned about the comparative information about schools performance that is available to parents. Parents are entitled to meaningful information when choosing a school for their child or to be reassured that their school is continuing to do a good job.

Parents need to be able to compare schools so that they can make the best possible choice for their child. If a school's results are consistently behind results from other schools, even if there is only one school serving a community, surely a community should have that right to know this so that they can press for change, improvement and the necessary resources?

We know a great deal about inputs into schools; for example, classroom, remedial and home–school liaison teachers, grants for computers, science and library books. However, by contrast we have virtually no evidence on what difference these inputs have made on outcomes for children. Schools must be able to compare results that they have achieved for children and share good practice. Schools do make a difference. Good schools make more of a difference. There is a greater need for the service to be more accountable and transparent.

NPC offers a range of services for parents and parents' associations. The services include a helpline and information service. NPC is an accredited training centre (FETAC) and runs many courses, workshops and public talks and lectures for parents. NPC runs a national network for parents through county branches and regional forums.

The NPC in the Future

Recent feedback from parents indicates that parents believe that the NPC is for every parent, for parents in special circumstances, for parents' associations, and also for others who have a "stake" in primary education. Parents include primary and pre-school parents and guardians, parents who may experience special challenges, such as lone parents and refugee parents. Others who have a stake in primary education include the Department of Education and Science, principals and teachers.

NPC is currently modernising to meet the identified needs of parents and to make the organisation more flexible and more responsive. NPC is hoping to open its doors to individuals as well as parents' associations. Our aim is to have an inclusive and flexible NPC, where parents of primary and pre-school children can easily get involved in the national organisation for parents.

For further information, contact the National Parents Council Primary, 12 Marlborough Court, Dublin 1; NPC helpline: 01-8874477; E-mail: info@npc.ie; Website: www.npc.ie.

Chapter 10

BURNING ISSUES IN SCHOOLS

BULLYING

There is no doubt that in recent years bullying, harassment and intimidation have become major issues in the public awareness in many walks of life, and schools as usual are no exception to general trends in society. There was always a certain amount of bullying in schools, but rarely to the extent that it was considered a serious issue on a large scale. Whether there is more bullying than there used to be; or whether the bullying that was always there has greatly increased in severity; or whether people are more thin-skinned than they used to be; or whether victims are more inclined to complain rather than suffer in silence; or whether the media has highlighted the issue more; or whether those in authority are now more ready than before to respond to such matters; or whether it is a combination of all these and other factors, the fact remains that bullying in schools, and on the way to and from school, is now a matter of concern for parents, pupils, their teachers and school management.

Although bullying takes place at all levels, it is usually only a major health and safety issue in second-level schools. The bullying that takes place in primary schools is certainly unpleasant for the sufferers and most distressing for their parents, but that is usually as far as it goes; happily it is still rare for there to be any serious consequences, other than the misery and unhappiness of the victim. This is not to trivialise the issue by any means, but occasionally in second-level schools, severe physical injury and psychological consequences can result. This seldom happens in primary schools, although it is not unknown.

Quite apart from this, bullying today can take new and insidious forms that were unknown in the past. Traditionally, bullying took the form of physical attacks on a pupil's person or property, or psychological attacks such as being excluded, name-calling, belittling and so forth, the former category being seen as mainly the preserve of boys, the latter of girls, although this distinction is far less the case than it used to be. A new type of bullying, widespread enough to have its own name among teachers — "e-bullying", using the ubiquitous technology of the e-mail and the text message — is now also prevalent, although much less so in primary than in second-level schools. Irrespective of its form, bullying is now a source of unhappiness for many pupils, a source of legitimate concern for their parents and hence a potential legal issue for their schools. This is not simply an issue in Ireland; other countries also report an increase in reported cases of bullying both in society generally and in schools.

Bullying is normally seen as a health and safety issue rather than a simple issue of school discipline, and there is now a substantial, and growing, body of literature on the topic, but all definitions agree that the problem is many-faceted, deep-seated, difficult to eradicate and an issue for management as well as individual teachers to tackle. There is also a general agreement that both the bully and the victim of bullying need support.

When the fact that bullying was a cause of concern in Irish schools became apparent, the response of the DES was to require the board of management of each recognised school to put in place a policy on dealing with bullying in its school. This was a welcome start, but more than mere policy-making needs to be done by a school to address the problem in schools where it is an issue. (There seems to be a general perception among teachers that the problem *is* a growing one.) Courses for teachers on detecting and dealing with bullying, as part of their in-service training, are now also becoming available, but much more in this line needs to be done.

Although bullying is, correctly, seen as a health and safety issue, it is different from other such issues in that it is frequently difficult to detect. Most safety issues in schools arise from factors such as dangerous floors or playgrounds, defective equipment, overcrowding, unsuitable and dangerous games and the like, and are at least easily identifiable, whatever about being easily soluble. Bullying is usually different, in that detection is often the biggest problem. This is particularly true of the non-physical or psychological forms, which do not leave any tangible or visible results for the teacher or parent to focus on. Another difficulty is that for various reasons children (and also adults) who are bullied very frequently find it a source of personal shame, as if they themselves were somehow to blame for their treatment, and so they find it difficult to complain. Frequently their shocked parents and teachers will find that the bullying has persisted for an appreciable time, and the child has endured weeks or even months of unhappiness, before the matter comes to the attention of any adult. This is exacerbated by the deep-seated culture of most schools in which tale-telling is frowned upon. All these factors combine to distinguish bullying as a separate issue from other issues of health and safety.

School supervision and discipline can go a long way towards dealing with bullying, particularly where the bullying is of a physical nature, but unless the bully (or bullies, for it is often a group activity) are caught in the act, it can be difficult, without physical signs, to establish that bullying is taking place at all. In cases where it is the word of one child against another or, even worse, against a group of others, most teachers will find great difficulty in taking action without corroborative evidence of some sort. It is a particular feature of bullying, and one that makes it a particularly insidious and intractable problem, that such corroboration is generally hard to find. This is something that parents often find difficult to understand. It is entirely natural and understandable that parents have no difficulty in taking their own child's word that he or she is being bullied, but they often have difficulty in accepting that the school needs something in the way of supporting evidence before any action can be taken. Teachers, who have more experience of dealing with children than any one parent, are always cautious about reacting in haste to allegations by one child against another, for they have experience of children's capacity to exaggerate events. They also have a duty to treat all the children in an even-handed way, which makes them slow to react without evidence. When a parent wants and demands an instant, unequivocal response, this can be a cause of friction between home and school.

Bullying can take place in almost any location where children congregate: the classroom, the playground, in corridors, in lavatories and washrooms, on the way to and from school, in the course of otherwise innocuous games. It can, and does, also take many forms. The definition proposed by the DES is comprehensive, although such a many-headed social phenomenon is difficult to capture in any definition:

> Bullying is repeated aggression, verbal, psychological or physical, conducted by an individual or group against others.

The DES has required for some time that schools incorporate an anti-bullying policy in their codes of behaviour. Policies on their own are of no use without a programme of implementation, and so schools also endeavour to raise an awareness among the school community of the problem, its potential seriousness, and the need for the whole community to tackle it. One thing that is established is that bullying must be addressed in a co-operative way by staff, pupils, parents and management, if there is to be any likelihood of success in dealing with it.

Given that children are notoriously reluctant to complain that they are being bullied, many schools try to create a "telling community" within the school, to encourage pupils to report when they themselves, or someone else, is a victim of the bully. They frequently provide parents with a check-list of tell-tale symptoms and signs of bullying to look out for, to alert them to oddities of their child's behaviour that may indicate that something is amiss. Here is an example is one such check-list drawn up by an infants' school; some schools use longer lists:

Possible Signs of Bullying in a Child

- Being frightened of going to the playground.

- Being unwilling to go to school.

- School work disimproving over time.

- Having clothes torn or books destroyed.

- Becoming withdrawn, starting to stammer.

- Having unexplained bruises, scratches, cuts.

- Refusing to say what's wrong.

- Giving improbable excuses to explain any of the above.

From the legal point of view, schools have to treat bullying as a health and safety issue, and teachers have to address it as part of their general duty to care for their charges, as outlined in Chapter 3. Given its widespread nature, and the growth of knowledge in society generally in recent years about bullying and its many damaging consequences, it is by now an identifiable and predictable hazard of school life of which teachers should be aware, and should be identified as such in the school safety statement and elsewhere, and counteracted at every opportunity.

MAINTAINING DISCIPLINE

Most parents probably conceive the purpose of school discipline as a means of maintaining order and control in the classroom to enable the teachers to teach and the pupils to learn. There are however other reasons why a school is required to maintain discipline and control. We have already seen (see Chapter 3) that school discipline is an important means through which the safety of pupils is secured, but another point not to be forgotten is that school discipline provides a form of learning in itself, equipping pupils with valuable life-skills that will enable them to progress successfully through the education system and into the world of work. The ultimate goal is self-discipline in later life, but like other accomplishments this has to be attained through practice and training. Discipline in school is therefore a significant matter in itself. While most pupils come to school already familiar with orderly systems in their homes, a minority do not, and expect to behave in school as they are used to behaving outside school. Since this is clearly impossible in the context of a school, where a population equivalent in many cases to that of a small town spends five days each week within a relatively confined space, and where good order, regulation and control are therefore essential, the topic of disciplining and controlling pupils is an area of legitimate parental interest and sometimes concern.

In the Irish education system, it has been generally accepted that a teacher's authority to control and discipline the pupils, and to enforce this discipline through reasonable sanctions, comes from a number of sources. It is, as we have seen in Chapter 3, part of the teacher's general duty of care, a means of guarding pupils against foreseeable risks, of which the risk of injury caused by the misbehaviour of their fellow pupils is undoubtedly one. Thus unacceptable behaviours such as dangerous or inappropriate games, bullying or fighting are all open to disciplinary procedures. Since the teacher stands in the place of the parent, and since parents are entitled to exercise discipline and control in respect of their children, the law holds that the teacher also has the right to exercise discipline and control in respect of the children that they teach, both to ensure safety and also to ensure conditions for teaching and learning. It is important that parents understand that teachers have both the right and duty to ensure that there is an efficient disciplinary system in operation both in the school and on school-related activities. School discipline operates in the classroom, on the school premises generally, on out-of-school activities such as tours and outings and on after-school activities such as games. Teachers are also entitled to exercise their disciplinary authority in relation to incidents that happen on occasions (such as the way to and from school) that may affect the school or a member of the school community; an incident of bullying or fighting on the way home from school would be an example of this.

In the relatively recent past, school discipline, especially in primary schools, was quite an informal business. Few schools had written rules, and there was an unwritten understanding that teachers were entitled to enforce reasonable rules by means of reasonable sanctions reasonably applied; everyone accepted this and disputes between schools and homes were relatively few. (Such disputes as there were usually related to the issue of corporal punishment, now a thing of the past.) This has greatly changed in recent years. The whole teacher–pupil–parent relationship has been greatly formalised, and school discipline as an element of that relationship has also been far more structured than formerly.

The Education (Welfare) Act 2000, is in essence, as we have seen (in Chapter 8) a new school attendance act, but it also addresses matters relating to school discipline. Section 23 obliges the board of management of a recognised school to prepare a code of behaviour for the students; parents among others have to be consulted in drawing this up. The code has to set out the standards of behaviour that each pupil must observe and the measures that the school proposes to take to deal with recalcitrant pupils. It must also state the procedures to be used before a student may be either suspended or expelled. (Formal expulsions from a national school are virtually unknown, but suspension is an option for serious breaches of school discipline.) Before a child is registered in a school, the principal is obliged to give the parent a copy of this code; the purpose of this is that the parents should be able to inform themselves of matters relating to the disciplinary system of the school before committing their child to the school as a pupil. Parents should take the time to read this before they finally enrol their child. This is important, as a parent will be held in law to have accepted the disciplinary system in force in the school once they make the decision to avail of that school. The school is entitled to require the parents to confirm in writing that the code of behaviour is acceptable to them and that they will make "all reasonable efforts" to ensure that their child complies with the code; therefore it is important that parents read the code before they sign up to it.

What if a parent wants to enrol the child in the school but is unwilling to sign the declaration of acceptance? In that case, the school is entitled to decline to register the child as a student at the school. The parent or the pupil is entitled to be given a copy of the code of behaviour by the principal on demand.

It is customary for the standards of behaviour to be observed by pupils to be reduced to the form of school rules. Some of these will clearly be aimed at creating and maintaining safety throughout the school; others deal with matters of punctuality, homework, dress code and such like. There will be a reason for every one of these rules, and parents who take the trouble to find out the reasons and explain them to their children are doing a favour to everyone in the school community and particularly to their own children.

A school must set out the sanctions that it proposes to use to deal with instances of pupil misbehaviour. They usually are placed in a list, ranging from the mildest (usually a verbal reprimand or piece of advice), in ascending order of severity and including such items as extra work, referral to the school principal, loss of privileges, detention during a break or after school and a written or oral complaint to the parent, right up to and including suspension from school, which would normally be the most severe. Schools usually like to communicate with the parents earlier rather than later with the hope of reaching a solution, as the desire is to solve the problem rather than to impose sanctions. There is now an obligation on schools to report long-term suspensions or frequent short suspensions to the education welfare officer assigned to the school, to enable that officer to liaise with the parents with a view to addressing the difficulties that the child is experiencing that may cause or contribute to the misbehaviour.

COMPLAINTS PROCEDURE

A parent who wishes to make a complaint should in the first place speak with the class teacher with a view to resolving the problem. Where the parent is unable to resolve the complaint with the class teacher, she/he should approach the principal with a view to re-solving it. If the complaint is still unresolved, the parent should raise the matter with the chairperson of the board of management. If the parent is still dissatisfied with the outcome, the complaint must be put in writing to the chairperson of the board of man-agement. At this stage, the issue is at the second stage of a five-stage procedure and further details may be obtained from the De-partment or National Parents Council.

The 1998 Act put in place a grievance procedure (in the form of sections 28 and 29) to enable a parent who is unhappy with their dealings with the school to have this unhappiness vented. The section 29 procedures relate to appeals against expulsions, long suspensions or refusals to admit students to schools. Of these, only refusals to admit are of much relevance to primary schools, and this matter (of admission to school) has already been dealt with in Chapter 2. Section 28 is likely to be much more rele-vant in this context. Very briefly, it provides that a parent may appeal to the board of management against a decision of a teacher or where the parent has a grievance in relation to the school. Al-though the section opens by stating that the Minister may pre-scribe procedures to enable this process to take place, at the time of writing this has never been done, although the Act has been in effect for four years. (However, it is understood that the process of drafting and publishing these procedures may be at last about to take place.) The board is required to take whatever action is ap-propriate to determine the appeal or resolve the grievance. Thus for example a parent who felt that his or her child had been wrongly sanctioned in school can appeal either the decision or the sanction to the board of management, and expect to have the mat-ter at issue looked into and, if appropriate, modified or corrected. In these situations, the board is required to act with scrupulous fairness in investigating the complaint, as it owes duties of fair-ness not only to both the child and its parents but also to its em-ployees, the teachers.

Until recently, an appeal to the board of management (and in the most exceptional circumstances to the patron) was the only prescribed recourse open to a parent who was unhappy with the operation of the school, short of removing the child entirely. Since 1 May 2004, however, there is another form of redress open, although one of relatively limited application. This is a referral to the Ombudsman for Children, an office created by the Ombudsman for Children Act 2002. This Act gives children and their parents or guardians a right to refer to the Ombudsman for investigation an administrative action, taken by a school, voluntary hospital or public body, that has or may have adversely affected a child. However, the process of drafting these procedures is in train, and a discussion draft was given a limited circulation in 2004. The powers of the Ombudsman are to investigate and to report the findings to the Oireachtas (and in the case of investigations into the actions of schools, to the DES). The Ombudsman has discretion as to whether or not to take up a reference, and may not do so unless the process of appeal to the board of management as provided for in section 28 of the 1998 Act has been resorted to and exhausted, and as the reference must relate to the discharge by a school of its functions under section 9 of that Act, it is unclear whether a matter relating to school discipline may come within the ambit of such a reference, as school discipline is not dealt with in section 9. The Ombudsman may, having carried out a preliminary investigation, decide to discontinue the investigation in prescribed circumstances, and is precluded entirely from investigating in certain others. (See the Appendix at the end of the book.)

GENDER BALANCE IN THE TEACHING PROFESSION

Co-education was for a long time a contentious issue. It was dealt with in the context of child development in Chapter 4. However, another gender-related issue has recently become a cause of some concern in Ireland: the increasingly lopsided gender balance in the teaching profession itself. Of the 25,913 teachers in the profession in 2003/2004 only 4,537 (17.5 per cent) were male. The proportion has been in steady decline in the last 30 years and this is set to continue as the age profile of male teachers is older and an examination of the intake into teacher training colleges shows the same trend.

Whether or not this phenomenon is worthy of discussion or concern to parents in general, it is a trend that the INTO and the DES are acutely aware of and have been researching and debating for some time. Of concern is the balance in the work environment; of providing children with role models of both sexes; of protecting the status and conditions associated with primary teaching; of stereotyping and the content and emphasis of the curriculum.

It is clear that further research is needed to determine why more females than males see it as an attractive career, why more females than males qualify for entry into teacher training and whether the imbalance has no or minimal impact on the experience or outcomes for pupils.

An interesting feature of the statistics is that while fewer than 20 per cent of the teachers are male, they represent 49 per cent of principals; and while 20 per cent of female teachers hold positions of principal, deputy principal, vice principal or assistant principal, almost half of all the male teachers hold one of these positions. As a consequence, the salary of the average male teacher (at €49,700) was €7,000 greater than the salary for the average female teacher (DES statistics).

Considering the fact that there are gender quotas on boards of management and interview boards, there may be some justification in having quotas for teachers also. In a poll conducted amongst its members by the INTO in 2003/04, 74 per cent of respondents were in favour of positive action measures to increase the numbers of males entering primary teaching. In guidelines issued to boards of management in recruiting teachers, interviewers are advised of their obligations in regard to the Employment Equality Act (1998) (Management Board Members' Handbook, 2004):

> (vi) No question shall be asked nor information sought in any form (from a candidate) which might be construed as being discriminatory on grounds of sex, of marital status, e.g. questions in regard to sporting interests and skills which would favour men rather than women applicants, or vice versa.

(vii) In the selection of staff for boys' only and girls' only schools, special care should be taken to ensure that both male and female applicants are given equal opportunity to present themselves as suitable and that questions put should not give the impression that the Board has a preconceived view of the suitability of either a man or a woman for a particular post.

If this situation is to be addressed it has to be done at second-level as students are preparing to make further education and career choices.

DIVERSITY IN PRIMARY EDUCATION

We are constantly being told that we now live in a multicultural, multiracial society and the census of 2002 gives a good overview of the changes not only in the resident population but also in the profile of those who have chosen to come and live and work here. By April 2004 the total population rose to over 4 million inhabitants the highest recorded since 1871 and the population increase alone from 2003 to 2004 was 64,900. Immigration, having peaked in 2002 at 66,900, fell back to 50,100 in 2004. If we look at immigration figures for the years 1996 to 2002 we can see the numbers of children in the school-going age 0–14.

Year	Number of Immigrants into Ireland Age 0–14
1996	6,600
1997	6,400
1998	7,200
1999	6,300
2000	5,000
2001	5,400
2002	5,300

In terms of religion, while the great majority of Irish people describe themselves as Roman Catholic, the proportion of the population describing themselves as Catholics actually dropped from

91.6 per cent to 88.4 per cent in the interval between 1991 and 2002, despite the fact that the actual number of self-described Catholics rose from 3.32 million in 1991 to 3.46 million in 2002.

Religion	1981	2002
Total	3,443,405	3,917,203
Roman Catholic	3,204,476	3,462,606
Church of Ireland	95,366	115,611
Presbyterian	14,255	20,582
Methodist	5,790	10,033
Jewish	2,127	1,790
Other Stated	10,843	89,233
No Religion	39,572	138,264
Not Stated	70,976	79,094

This is because of the total increase in population and the increase in those who describe themselves as belonging to other religions or none. While the majority of parents in Ireland will probably retain a preference for denominational education, the greatest demand for alternatives comes from those who seek a multi-denominational option and those seeking education through the medium of Irish (see Chapter 5).

The Education Act 1998 specifically refers to the objective to promote "equality of access . . . and shall have regard to the resources available", and "the need to reflect the diversity of educational services provided in the State". In addition, the board of management is compelled to carry out its functions having regard to "the principles and requirements of a democratic society and have respect and promote respect for the diversity of values, beliefs, traditions, languages and ways of life in society".

The Equality Authority was set up to promote equality of opportunity and to combat discrimination. Both the Employment Equality Act and the Equal Status Act prohibit discrimination on nine grounds, which are gender, family status, marital status, sexual orientation, religion, age, race, disability and membership of the Traveller community.

The DES has many initiatives in place to address the growing diversity of the school population, including guidelines on Traveller Education; Promoting Anti-Racism and Inter-Culturalism in Education; Promoting Gender Equality; and many programmes to tackle disadvantage and the needs of those with special educational needs. Readers or interested groups with specific queries in relation to equality of access and participation would be well advised to contact the Department directly to obtain more detailed information.

Diversity within a school and diversity among schools are both legitimate aspects of the principle of diversity; it is not expected that all schools should be exactly the same. If there is to be a capacity not only to cope with different religions and values, there also must exist a space for different educational philosophies. The implementation of the curriculum allows a certain scope for different educational programmes to be incorporated depending on the ethos of the school (see Chapters 2 and 5 for more on school ethos).

The degree to which it is desirable or possible to provide for the whole spectrum of religious and cultural groups that now exist in Ireland is dependent on the resources made available and the priorities for those competing resources. Inclusion is more than just access, it is also about recognition of differences between people and groups in society and valuing, accommodating and celebrating these differences. Many studies show that young children accept difference readily when experienced at a young age. The inclusion of pupils of different backgrounds and with different abilities can be an enriching experience for all if properly planned and resourced.

As discussed in Chapter 7, when a pupil with a disability is enrolled into a mainstream school, resources and supports must be put in place to allow that pupil equal participation in as far as is possible. In the same way, children who are foreign nationals or asylum-seekers may have additional needs, for example in terms of English language support and cultural understanding, to prevent exclusion and isolation in the classroom. Similarly, understanding the culture, traditions, values and history of the Traveller community is essential to the successful integration of Traveller children in mainstream schooling.

While many of those involved in primary education are pioneers in leading the discussion and action on many of these issues, school generally reflect the society in which they function. If schools are to be more inclusive, they need the support of pupils, parents and the community in accepting and welcoming minorities. There may be a need for some discussion, for example in dealing with apprehension and lack of information.

If a particular school in a town or community is progressive and fair about actively promoting inclusion of minorities, it is wrong for neighbouring schools to relinquish their obligations in terms of not discriminating on the grounds of race, religion or membership of the Traveller community. The "inclusive school" then becomes known as the school attended by those who are "different" — whether they are Travellers, immigrants, children with disabilities, the socially disadvantaged, etc. — and parents who might be prejudiced against such groups will avoid sending their children there. This can create a vicious circle, where the already limited resources in such schools are further put under strain, with the result that those schools that try hardest are putting themselves at a disadvantage.

If diversity is to be promoted across all schools, resources need to be provided not only in terms of physical resources but also in personnel to conduct research and develop programmes that remove barriers and increase full participation. True inclusiveness can only work if the general culture of education throughout the country is positively disposed to it, and is seen to be so in practice.

FURTHER READING

(Note: This is a general reading list. Some chapters also include references specific to the issues discussed therein. There are just two references here for Department of Education and Science publications; all Departmental publications are now available online at their website: http://www.education.ie/servlet/blobservlet/des_publication_listing.htm)

Catholic Primary School Management Association (2004), *Management Board Members' Handbook*, CPSMA.

Coolahan, John (1980), *Irish Education: History and Structure*, Institute of Public Administration.

Department of Education and Science, *Developing a School Plan: Guidelines for Primary Schools*, Stationery Office.

Department of Education and Science, *Rules for National Schools*, Stationery Office.

Drudy, S. and Uí Catháin, M. (1999), *Schools and Society in Ireland*, Gill and Macmillan.

Fanning, B., Veale, A., and O'Connor, D. (2001), *Beyond the Pale: Asylum-Seeking Children and Social Exclusion in Ireland*, Irish Refugee Council.

Furlong, C. and Monahan, L. (2000), *School Culture and Ethos: Cracking the Code*, Marino Institute of Education.

Gilsenan, Brian, *The Essential Parent's Guide to the Primary School Years*, Primary ABC.

Hopkins, David and Reynolds, David (1994), *School Development in an Era of Change*, Cassell.

INTO/Equality Authority (2004), *The Inclusive School*, Proceedings of the Joint Conference of the Irish National Teachers Organisation and the Equality Authority.

Lodge, Anne and Lynch, Kathleen (2004), *Diversity at School*, Equality Authority.

Mahon, O. (2000), *Users Guide to the Education Act*, Clare Education Centre.

National Council for Curriculum and Assessment (for Department of Education and Science) (1999), *Your Child's Learning: Primary School Curriculum, Guidelines for Parents*, Stationery Office.

National Parents Council (Primary) (Revised 2004), *Working Effectively as a Parents' Association*, NPC.

Smyth, Emer (1999), *Do Schools Differ?* ESRI/Oak Tree Press.

RESOURCES

Further information may be obtained from the following sources. Please note that contact details for other organisations are provided at appropriate places in the book; please refer to the index if you cannot find the organisation you are looking for here.

Department of Education and Science,
Marlborough Street,
Dublin 1.
Tel: 01-8896400
Website: www.education.ie

Department of Education and Science,
Primary Branch,
Cornamaddy,
Athlone,
Co. Westmeath.
Tel: 090-6483600

Department of Education and Science,
Planning Section,
Portlaoise Road,
Tullamore,
Co. Offaly.
Tel: 0506-21363

Irish National Teachers Organisation (INTO),
Vere Foster House,
35 Parnell Square,
Dublin 1.
Tel. 01-8047700
Website: www.into.ie

National Association of Principals & Deputy Principals (NAPD),
46 Lower Leeson St.
Dublin 2.
Tel: 01-6627025
Website: www.napd.ie

National Council for Curriculum and Assessment (NCCA),
24 Merrion Square,
Dublin 2.
Tel: 01-6617177
www.ncca.ie

National Educational Welfare Board,
16-22 Green Street,
Dublin 7.
Tel: Lo-Call 1890-363666
Website: www.newb.ie

National Parents Council Primary,
12 Marlborough Court,
Dublin 1.
NPC Helpline: 01-8874477
E-mail: info@npc.ie
Website: www.npc.ie

National Council for Special Education,
Trim,
Co. Meath.
Tel: 046-9436666

National Educational Psychological Service,
Frederick Court,
North Frederick Street,
Dublin 1.
Tel: 01-8892700

Special Education Support Service,
c/o Laois Education Centre,
Block Road,
Portlaoise,
Co. Laois.
Tel: 0502-72402/72409
E-mail: info@sess.ie
Website: www.sess.ie

National Disability Authority,
25 Clyde Road,
Dublin 4.
Tel: 01-6080400
Website: www.nda.ie

One Parent Exchange and Network,
Unit 19,
Greendale Ctr.
Dublin 5.
Tel 01-8320264
Website: www.oneparent.ie

Children's Rights Alliance,
13 Harcourt St,
Dublin 2
Tel. 01-4054823
www.childrensrights.ie

National Children's Office,
1st Floor St. Martins House,
Waterloo Road,
Dublin 4.
Tel. 01-2420000
Website: www.nco.ie

Ombudsman for Children
Tel: 1890 654 654
E-mail: oco@oco.ie
Website: www.oco.ie

www.scoilnet.ie

www.edunet.ie

Appendix

THE OMBUDSMAN FOR CHILDREN ACT 2002
A Summary for Parents of its Important Points

Note: This summary is intended to inform parents of the parts of the Act that are likely to be of importance to them, and so all other parts of the Act are omitted. It is not, and is not intended to be, a legal interpretation, and anyone who may need such an interpretation should consult a lawyer. Since this book is about education, only those parts of the Act that relate in one way or another to education are included, and the parts relating to voluntary hospitals and public bodies have been omitted. For convenience, the summary is in the form of numbered points.

1. The Act was passed on 1 May 2002 and came into effect on 1 May 2004.

2. It establishes a new office in Ireland, the Ombudsman for Children. (The word "Ombudsman" is gender-neutral, and the first Ombudsman is a woman, Ms Emily Logan.)

3. The Ombudsman is appointed by the President, holds office for six years, may only serve one term, may not simultaneously hold any other position or any elected office and may only be removed by the Oireachtas following a process similar to impeachment. The purpose of these provisions is to ensure the independence of the office.

4. The Ombudsman's primary function is to promote the rights and welfare of children, and in order to do this is empowered to advise ministers, encourage various bodies and institutions, publicise the topic of Children's Rights, highlight relevant issues and consult with groups representing children's opinions, and also to raise awareness of an important instrument in International Law, the

United Nations Convention on the Rights of the Child, which is
the source of the office of Ombudsman and is intended to be the
equivalent for children of the Universal Declaration of Human
Rights of 1948, which is probably the most important statement of
human rights in history.

5. As well as promoting children's rights and building an awareness
    of them, the Ombudsman is also empowered to investigate com-
    plaints about administrative actions that have or may have ad-
    versely affected the interests of a child and may have been taken
    on any of a number of improper grounds. At present the Om-
    budsman is confined to investigating actions taken by or on behalf
    of a voluntary hospital, a public body or a recognised school, al-
    though the intention is that administrative acts of any body, public
    or private, that may have adversely affected the interests of a child
    will eventually be subject to the Ombudsman's scrutiny. However,
    this will probably require a constitutional amendment.

6. A "child" means anyone under 18, which is in fact the age of ma-
    jority in Ireland. The word "school" includes the board of man-
    agement, principal, teachers and other staff. An "action" includes
    a decision, an omission or a failure to act; "function" includes
    both powers and duties, and "the Minister" is the Minister for
    Health and Children, not Education, as this is not an education
    act, although it does have significant implications for schools,
    teachers, parents and children.

7. In relation to schools, the kinds of actions that may be investi-
    gated are those related to the administration of the school, and
    must be in connection with the school functions as set out in sec-
    tion 9 of the Education Act 1998. This means that the remit of the
    Ombudsman to investigate complaints relating to children's
    rights is by no means as broad as might be thought.

8. To qualify for a reference to the Ombudsman, the action must
    have been one that has (or may have) adversely affected the child,
    and also must have been for some reason improperly taken, such
    as being improperly discriminatory or having been taken without
    proper authority; the precise grounds that may make the action
    flawed are set out in section 9 of the Act. However — and this is
    most important — the Ombudsman cannot act unless the local

appeals procedures set out in section 28 of the 1998 Act (and dealt with in Chapter 10) have been tried and have failed.

9. Not only can a child complain about an administrative action, so can others acting on his or her behalf. A parent, and any other person who has a sufficient relationship with the child, which specifically includes a professional relationship, may also complain, but it is important to note that there must be a sufficient relationship of whatever sort to give the complainant the standing to make the complaint. (The Ombudsman is the judge whether the relationship is adequate for this purpose or not.) The Ombudsman has however the discretion to carry out an investigation without any formal complaint being lodged if it appears that this would be appropriate in the circumstances.

10. The Ombudsman first carries out a preliminary examination, and then must decide whether to carry out a full-scale investigation or not. (Obviously this decision would have to be made on whatever facts were disclosed by the preliminary examination.) Even if the Ombudsman decides to investigate, she may discontinue the investigation if this seems appropriate, and there are criteria set out in the Act to enable the Ombudsman to come to this conclusion. (For instance, if so much time has passed since the action was taken as to make any useful redress impossible, then the investigation would be pointless, and the Ombudsman could decide not to proceed.)

11. There are certain actions that the Ombudsman is not allowed to investigate at all; these are also set out in detail in the Act. There are several of these exclusions, most of which would not arise in the context of a school. The relevant ones would be where a legal case had already been commenced in relation to the action in question; where the child has a legal right to appeal to a court; where the child has some other right of appeal besides a court action; where the complaint would relate to the results of a public examination in a school; if the complaint was not made within two years of the action being taken; or if the action took place before the Act commenced, i.e. 1 May 2004.

12. If the Ombudsman, having received a complaint, decides not to investigate it or to discontinue an investigation, a statement of

the reasons for so doing must be sent to the complainant, and to any other person considered appropriate to receive it.

13. If the Ombudsman does conduct an investigation, a statement of results must be sent to the school, the DES, the person who is alleged to have authorised the action and to any other person considered appropriate to be sent this statement, as well as the complainant.

14. If, after an investigation, the Ombudsman believes that the action did adversely affect a child, she is empowered to recommend that the action be further considered, that measures be taken to repair the damage to the child or that the reasons for the decision be given to the Ombudsman, if necessary within a specific time.

15. The Ombudsman may not make a finding that is critical of anyone without having given that person an opportunity to give their side of the story and to reply to any criticism.

16. The Ombudsman is obliged to lodge an annual report before the Houses of the Oireachtas in relation to functions performed during that year and may make whatever other reports as from time to time appear appropriate. No one can sue in defamation (i.e. libel and slander) on foot of any report issued by the Ombudsman.

17. In carrying out a preliminary examination (see point No. 10 above), the Ombudsman may require any person who holds useful information to furnish it, or to produce documents or things, or to attend at a hearing in relation to it, and that person must do so. Anyone who hinders or obstructs the Ombudsman will be treated as being in contempt.

18. Investigations by the Ombudsman must not be in public, and the Ombudsman has authority to set the procedures for conducting the investigation. The Ombudsman also has authority to decide whether any person involved in an investigation may have legal or other representation.

19. Any information disclosed, or documents or things handed over (see point No. 17 above) to the Ombudsman during an examination or an investigation shall not be disclosed other then where necessary for the purposes of the Act.

INDEX